The Relentlessly Practical Guide to Raising Serious Money

Proven Strategies for Nonprofit Organizations

THE RELENTLESSLY PRACTICAL GUIDE TO RAISING

SERIOUS MONEY

SECOND EDITION

PROVEN STRATEGIES FOR NONPROFIT ORGANIZATIONS

DAVID LANSDOWNE

Emerson
& Church

First printed February 2004

10 9 8 7 6 5 4 3 2 1

Printed in the United States of America

This text is printed on acid-free paper.

Copies of this book are available from the publisher at discount when purchased in quantity for boards of directors or staff.

Emerson & Church, Publishers
P.O. Box 338
Medfield, MA 02052
Tel. 508-359-0019
www.contributionsmagazine.com

Library of Congress Cataloging-in-Publication Data

Lansdowne, David.
    The relentlessly practical guide to raising serious money : proven strategies for nonprofit organizations / David Lansdowne.
        p. cm.
    ISBN 1-889102-19-9 (alk. paper)
        1. Fund raising. 2. Nonprofit organizations--Finance. I. Title

HV41.2.L357 2004
658.15'224--dc22   2003064313

CONTENTS

To Kathy

Relentless in her love and expression of character

ACKNOWLEDGMENT

The author is indebted to a host of great fund raising practitioners, from Harold Seymour to Thomas Broce to Jerold Panas, without whose insights, wisdom, and trailblazing, this book would not be possible.

PREFACE

Can a single book address all of your fund raising needs? Probably not, unless yours is a small organization.

Still, *The Relentlessly Practical Guide to Raising Serious Money* attempts to be all-encompassing in examining every major facet of fund raising.

By doing so, my goal is to provide you with solid footing, whether you're launching a capital campaign, conducting a special event, experimenting with the Internet, or weighing the merits of one fund raising method over another.

Any single method is worthy of an entire book. And of course there are scores of titles on specific areas such as annual giving, corporate philanthropy, grantwriting, and prospect research. I don't attempt to replicate these books here.

Instead, what *Relentless* offers is something more germaine to the generalist. You won't find minutiae in these pages, or ponderous case studies, or untenable theory.

What you will find is the very essence of what you must know to excel at raising money for your worthy cause.

--*David Lansdowne*

Also by David Lansdowne

FUND RAISING REALITIES EVERY BOARD MEMBER MUST FACE

A 1-Hour Crash Course on Raising Major Gifts
112 pp., Emerson & Church, Publishers
ISBN: 1889102105

If every board member of every nonprofit organization across America read this book, it's no exaggeration to say that millions upon millions of additional dollars would be raised.

How could it be otherwise when, after spending just *one* hour with this classic, board members everywhere would understand virtually everything they need to know about raising major gifts. Not more, not less. Just exactly what they need to do to be successful.

In his book, *Fund Raising Realities Every Board Member Must Face: A 1-Hour Crash Course on Raising Major Gifts for Nonprofit Organizations*, David Lansdowne has distilled the essence of major gifts fund raising, put it in the context of 47 "realities," and delivered it in unfailingly clear prose.

Nothing about this book will intimidate board members. It is brief, concise, easy to read and free of all jargon. Further, it is a work that motivates, showing as it does just how doable raising big money is.

The appeal of *Fund Raising Realities* is that Lansdowne addresses every important principle and technique of fund raising, and explains them in a succinct way board members will grasp immediately. In other words, *Fund Raising Realities* puts everyone on a level playing field - board member with board member, and board member with staff.

Emerson
& Church
PUBLISHERS

1

The 16 Best Pieces of Fund Raising Advice

The more things change, the more they remain the same. Isn't it strange that after more than eight decades of fund raising, after literally thousands of workshops and seminars, after innumerable barrels of ink have washed over countless books, that after all this, successful fund raising can be distilled down to a mere 16 tenets.

But, come to think of it, maybe that shouldn't be surprising. There are, after all, only 10 commandments, a mere seven Wonders of the World, and just one Golden Rule.

Granted, you can't illuminate every aspect of fund raising, every nuance and shade, every subtle underpinning in just a handful of essentials. But it is safe to say, if you abide by each of the principles below, you will almost always experience a startling degree of success.

1) GET STARTED NOW
It's a fact of life that whenever we have plenty of time to

do something, it seldom gets done. This is especially true in fund raising. While most of us decry pressure -- who likes to be told to "Do it now!" -- any campaign, small or large, requires timetables, report meetings, and deadlines. They are the antidote to procrastination, the device that moves a reluctant volunteer from procrastinator to solicitor.

Without an adhered-to schedule, your fund raising will stall, or worse, wither away. And, if you're advised to wait for a better time to begin your campaign, realize that when you've made your plans properly, that alone is the perfect time to begin.

2) ASK FOR A SPECIFIC GIFT

The need to ask for a specific gift is one of the most commonly misunderstood principles in fund raising. While many volunteers are willing to seek from prospects "any amount at all" or "whatever you can give," when told to request a specific dollar figure they almost always balk.

Yet, without the mention of a figure, the prospect dangles, forced to guess at the solicitor's intentions, "I wonder if he means $50 or $500?" This uncertainty — and discomfort — is eliminated instantly by citing a specific amount.

Granted, you can only suggest the level and not insist upon it. But the figure carries great weight, raising the sights of the prospect and letting him or her know you've given careful thought to your campaign.

3) ASK ACCORDINGLY

Raising money by the multiplication table — attempting, for instance, to persuade 1,000 people to give $1,000 each — rarely if ever works.

Most prospects won't come up with that arbitrary amount; another contingent might want to, but can't afford it; still others will give you nothing. Worst of all, some who might be inclined to give you $10,000 will be discouraged from doing so. Rather than "averaging" and relying upon 100 percent participation, a far more realistic approach is to determine how many gifts of differing amounts you need to reach your goal.

This means carefully researching and rating your prospects, and developing a "gift table" to serve as a guide to your solicitations. After all, would you think it fair to be solicited for the very same amount as a prosperous entrepreneur?

4) GET THEM INVOLVED

Ideally, all organizations should be involving their constituencies at all times, and not merely when funds are needed.

To be sure, involvement has many faces. It can be big, like asking someone to serve on a nominating committee, or it can be small, like seeking a donor's advice or asking her to do something for you.

You will find, almost invariably, that the best trustees are those who are meaningfully involved. The same can be said for the most successful solicitors. And the best contributors are those who are involved in your effort from conception to victory.

One caveat: don't delude yourself into thinking you can rush a rich person on board and have him or her contribute significantly to your cause. Almost always, earning the trust and commitment of a major gift prospect is a slow, ongoing process, sometimes taking years.

5) DESCRIBE IT IN HUMAN TERMS

Whatever you're raising money for, strive to make your project personal for the potential donor. A library isn't merely a collection of books, it's a fertile place where young minds grow. Cancer research isn't sterile equipment and test tubes, it's the promise of a cure for someone engulfed by the disease.

15

A museum is for people, nature preserves are for people, restoring an historical site is for people.

With a little forethought and imagination, it won't be hard to translate your campaign into human terms, something people can connect to or feel warmly about.

6) DON'T COUNT ON PUBLICITY

Each year, thousands of organizations waste millions of dollars on materials of little or no value in raising money. Why the reliance on these crutches (for in reality that's what they are)?

First and foremost, people want to avoid the discomfort of looking a prospect in the eye and asking for a contribution. To avoid that dreaded task, people will go to almost any length. But there are other reasons too.

Perhaps those connected with your organization doubt the worthiness of the cause and seek assurance behind glossy brochures. Others may feel the printed word has magic and is therefore more effective than the spoken word. Still others may yearn to be part of a carefully constructed image of success. Whatever the reasons the sad truth is, publicity doesn't raise money. It never did, and it never will.

7) SEEK THE VERY BEST LEADERS

If there's one requirement for successful fund raising, it's strength at the top. No organization is ever stronger than its leadership, nor can it extend its constituency beyond the sphere of influence its leadership represents. Truly effective leaders are rare, of course, but they're always worth looking for and waiting for.

Si Seymour, author of *Designs for Fund Raising*, describes this special breed best: "They bring warmth and confidence to the cause. They have a way of attracting the interest and loyalty of effective and devoted lieutenants. They give the required amount of their talents and their time. They know what the committee system is for and how to use it. And, finally, by the example of their own words, deeds, and gifts, they help to set high standards of campaign performance. They never question the good faith of those with other views, and they never doubt the ultimate victory."

8) LOOK TO THYSELF, FIRST

In successful fund raising, the "rock in the pond" principle must prevail. An organization cannot expect others to invest in it until those closest to the center ante up. Solicitation should proceed, therefore, from the inside out, starting with the board and the institutional family and then spreading outward.

And always keep in mind that fund raising is subject to a law of diminishing returns — the wider the periphery, the greater the effort, the smaller the gift, and the higher the cost. This frequently makes board members squirm, for it can be their first collective realization that, on all prospect lists, their names come first.

9) LOOK 'EM IN THE EYE

The best way to raise money is to ask for it, and the best method to use is person-to-person, eyeball-to-eyeball contact. But how often this "first principle" is neglected by staff and volunteers. Inclement weather, aches and pains, too harried at the office, yesterday's failure, or even yesterday's big success — all these and a host of other excuses can prevent a reluctant fund raiser from making personal calls.

But no mistake will be as costly to you. The shopworn phrase, people give to people, fully applies. While a positive image in the prospect's mind will help, what really wins his or her contribution is the "ask," the personal entreaty of a friend or peer. Substantial gifts come from making personal calls. That's the plain and simple truth.

10) BE GRATEFUL, EVEN FOR SMALL GIFTS

The story goes that when Booker T. Washington was soliciting funds for Tuskegee Institute, he received in the mail one morning a crisp dollar bill from John D. Rockefeller.

Others may have scoffed or been irate at this token gesture, but not Washington. He wrote and duly thanked Rockefeller ... and he did more. At the end of the year he sent the tycoon a detailed accounting of what had been done with the dollar, penny by penny. Impressed, Rockefeller thereafter supported Washington's work in earnest.

11) HIRED GUNS CAN'T DO IT FOR YOU

Fund raising can't be hired out to paid professionals. As mentioned earlier, an institution cannot expect others to support it until those closest to the center do so — and at generous levels. Sad to say, there are no fund raising Lone Rangers who'll gallop into your community, deposit bags of gold, and ride off to the wild cheers of your board of trustees.

What reputable professionals will do, and won't do, is summed up best by John Schwartz, former president of the American Association of Fund Raising Counsel (now the Association of Fundraising Professionals).

They *will* identify the strengths and weakness of your organization; they *will* set up the conditions for action; they *will* predict costs and maintain budget controls; they *will* provide an overall plan; they *will* stimulate and organize top leaders to make them effective; they *will* be the first to tell you if you cannot do what you are trying to do.

They *will not* normally be active in the solicitation of contributions; they *will not* relieve top people of responsibilities in the fund raising effort; they *will not* take over, hire or fire staff; they *will not* give you any magic formula.

12) AIM YOUR FOCUS ON INDIVIDUALS

It's a fundamental error, for the majority of organizations, to focus on corporations and foundations and almost totally ignore individual prospects. By doing so, they restrict their efforts to about 10 percent of the philanthropic pie (individuals account for nearly 90 percent of all funds donated each year).

Why is this error so common? In no small measure because foundations and corporations are the easiest targets. They fully expect to be solicited. Foundations exist to award grants, and many businesses, as a cost of doing business, routinely allot monies for philanthropic causes. As a result, the hardest part of any fund raiser's job, the most feared one — namely, asking — is a foregone conclusion.

13) NURTURE PAST DONORS

How you treat donors after they give to you determines, in large part, whether they will give to you again. Treat them well and chances are they will give to you again ... and again.

Anyone who's been in the fund raising field for a while knows that past donors are an organization's best prospects. They have already expressed their trust in the most meaningful of ways — by parting with their hard-earned dollars. Thank them, respect them, involve them, keep them informed, and, most importantly, appeal to them often, and you'll be surprised at just how generously they'll respond.

14) FOCUS ON THEIR NEEDS, NOT YOURS

Despite the worthiness of your cause, or the multitude of people you help, there's no good reason why prospects should give you money just because you ask. More likely they'll give when they see a benefit for themselves.

Imagine your donors as customers. Would it be sensible to advertise the following? "Shop here, we need customers to stay in the black." Of course not. Customers aren't interested in helping a business prosper, they're interested in low prices, quality, convenience, service, and variety.

In sum, they're interested in what they need. By thinking of your donors as customers, you'll move away from your need to theirs, which will go a long way toward making your fund raising approach compelling.

15) ASK, BUT AS THE LAST STEP

The final, and not the first, step in fund raising is the solicitation of gifts. This may surprise those who think solicitation alone is fund raising. The practiced fund raiser knows that only when a series of earlier steps have been followed does asking come easily.

Before the actual solicitation comes planning, recruiting the right leaders, preparing your arguments, researching and rating your prospects, cultivating these people, and matching the right solicitor to the prospect.

Only when each of these steps has been accomplished, are you truly prepared for the actual solicitation, which then should be relatively easy.

At that point, you will have meaningfully involved your prospect, shared your vision and goals, and demonstrated their importance to the community if not to humankind.

16) KEEP IT SIMPLE

Keep in mind that, despite all principles and techniques, fund raising at heart is quite simple. As author Irving Warner succinctly puts it, "You raise money when you ask for it, preferably face to face, from the smallest possible number of people, in the shortest period of time, at the least expense."

2

Fund Raising Leadership

An organization's ability to raise money is almost always in direct proportion to the quality and commitment of its fund raising leadership.

Those that attract and retain able leadership prosper, while those that settle for lackluster trustees and volunteers usually languish.

It is common for organizations, especially when setting out to raise money, to bemoan their "weak boards." However, by then it's too late to scour the community for wealthy new members (who simply won't give that quickly anyway).

Instead, organizations should place a priority on *continually* strengthening their boards. This isn't to say all trustees should be wealthy, for other skills are also needed to govern.

But, if an organization relies on private contributions for its existence, then affluent persons with a concern for your mission *must* be sought out for leadership.

This essential task will be made easier by adhering to the suggestions that follow.

BE WATCHFUL

A high priority for the chief executive or development officer of any organization should be the constant watchfulness for promising trustees.

In fact, candidates who show potential should be ardently pursued. They are, after all, as important to you as major donors (a determined board can accomplish nearly any objective).

Some organizations recruit trustees without regard to their affluence or influence. And while there's nothing wrong with enlisting those who represent various constituencies, or those who bring special talents, don't expect them to have fund raising prowess. You'll still need your share of "clout carrying" board members if you hope to raise real money.

LOOK WITHIN

Generally, you will find fund raising leadership in the family, that is, within your board, advisory groups, and other natural constituencies. In fact, one reliable way of measuring your strength is to see whether you have on your board -- or somewhere within your organization -- a person who falls into one of the following groups:

❏ Individuals who have inherited money and a tradition of public service

❏ Self-made men and women who are newly rich and newly powerful

❏ Top professional managers of key corporations

❏ Respected and admired individuals in the community

An absence of leadership along these lines indicates that your organization isn't yet prepared for serious fund raising and some organizational shuffling may be in order.

INVOLVE FIRST

Most people don't like to be asked to "work for" or "give

to" an organization they know little about.

To the contrary, if you hope to inspire individuals to invest in your program, they must have the opportunity to be involved in its planning and operation. The fact is, people are more motivated to work for, and invest in, something they have helped to develop.

Of course, a simple way to encourage involvement is to invite a person to do something important for you -- something he or she is uniquely qualified for.

Then, too, there are formal approaches such as membership on advisory committees, one-on-one relationships involving the chief executive, and participation or attendance at special events.

Whatever your approach, involving prospects must be a continuous activity, not one engaged in only when money is on the line. Most prospects are smart enough to see through intensive courtship during fund raising.

THE BOARD'S ROLE

It only makes sense that trustees must serve in the forefront of any effort to raise money for a project they've reviewed, approved, and set in motion.

Granted, additional people will be needed as volunteer leaders and workers, but the role of the board -- the role of those who literally own the organization -- cannot be matched by any other group.

Trustees, if they are to be taken seriously, must set an example by making gifts that are generous and proportionate, by soliciting their peers and colleagues, by working to bring other people into the program, and by staying informed and enthusiastic about their organization.

QUALITIES TO LOOK FOR

What makes for strong fund raising leadership? There

are, in essence, four factors: affluence, influence, availability, and team spirit.

The most effective leader has the wherewithal to make a significant contribution. She's able to attract others to volunteer and to contribute. She's willing to give priority attention to your program. And she's able to accept professional direction without balking.

What about passion for the cause -- is this essential? Not necessarily, as it can be developed.

Fund raising leadership demands certain qualities, it's true. But what is equally required is genuine commitment and enthusiasm.

WHY LEADERS JOIN

What will prompt leaders to join your organization? To serve on your board and committees, to give you more than fleeting interest and token gifts?

First, because you ask them. How many people step forward and offer their services without being asked? Very few. But there other important reasons as well. You offer:

❑ Community recognition
❑ Opportunities for achievement and prestige
❑ Opportunities to solve important problems
❑ Camaraderie with other leaders
❑ A compelling and widely shared institutional vision
❑ Opportunities for personal and professional growth

To the extent you can offer any or all of the above, you will attract fund raising leadership.

DRAWN TO SUCCESS

While they may be popular in sports, underdogs don't fare nearly as well in fund raising. We are a people drawn to success, who like winning organizations.

Tell volunteers you're on your last legs, struggling to keep the doors open for another day, and chances are they'll stick around just long enough to say goodbye.

To attract individuals capable of genuine leadership in fund raising, you'll have to show evidence of your competence, stability, and reputation.

THE CHAIRPERSON IS PARAMOUNT

You can succeed without the perfect chairperson (or we'd all be in a mess). But choose the wrong man or woman, someone without a preponderance of the following traits, and your failure is nearly assured.

Look for a person who is:
- ❏ Experienced in fund raising
- ❏ Willing to make a pace-setting gift
- ❏ A persuasive solicitor
- ❏ Owed more favors than he owes
- ❏ Well-known and respected in the community
- ❏ Able to surround herself with loyal workers
- ❏ Accessible during your campaign

WHEN RECRUITING YOUR CHAIRPERSON

Once you've identified your chairperson of choice, call and make an appointment to see her. Don't state your purpose, if possible. Simply say it's a matter important enough to justify an hour of her time.

Moreover, plan to bring one or two other people with you. You'll be able to determine just who these people should be, assuming you've researched your prospective chairperson (perhaps the hospital's chief of staff is the right person or the local banker or the teen who's overcome the disease you fight).

During your visit, be concise. Relate the essentials of your project and why you feel your candidate should be chairperson. Outline the time commitment. Share the names of others with whom she would be working. Say when you expect to finish. And tell her how much the inner group has pledged so she'll know how much money is expected of her.

In most cases the individual will ask for time to think over your offer. Avoid the delay, if possible. Do everything you can to get an answer then and there. Remember, this is your one best chance at her; you may not get another.

DON'T FORCE IT

Whether your candidate accepts will be determined in part by how comfortable he feels with the mission and purpose of your organization.

You might have a stellar reputation, a respected staff, and unquestioned financial stability, but still not be able to attract certain people as volunteers. When this happens, the individual most likely feels that yours isn't a cause he can effectively advocate for.

In such a case, be grateful for his honesty. It's far better for the person to decline your invitation than to sign on and later decide to leave.

LEADERS NEED TRAINING TOO

The reluctance of many to join a fund raising team often stems from their fear of the process and their lack of training.

By adopting the following strategies, you can help your volunteers overcome their hesitancy and be as effective as possible.

❑ Encourage your leaders to participate in the planning process, including the setting of fund raising goals and objectives

❑ Provide training that demonstrates the *how* of fund raising (the methodology) and the *why* (the principles)

❑ Use demonstrations and videotapes to reduce anxiety about making solicitation calls

❑ Team your leaders with an experienced volunteer or a staff member for solicitation visits

❑ Remind them as often as possible of the mission of your organization, and of the needs they're helping to meet.

HONORARY IS SOMETIMES USEFUL

Honorary chairpeople can be worthwhile for two reasons: to lend prestige and credibility to your project (especially if you're relatively unknown), and to put you in touch with potential donors who might not be approachable otherwise.

However, the presence of honorary chairpeople won't bring you sizable contributions. Prospects don't respond to letterheads; they respond to enthusiastic solicitors who make persuasive presentations.

One final note: don't expect these individuals to attend many meetings or solicit many prospects. Remember, their title is "honorary."

CO-CHAIRS CAN WORK

The absence of the ideal chairperson may lead you to two or even three people who together have the qualities you seek. Here's a case when co-chairs might be recruited and used successfully, assuming you skillfully coordinate the role and workload of each.

Another instance of effective co-chairpersons is when you recruit your ideal candidate and she's reluctant to take on sole responsibility. Then it can be very beneficial to offer her the co-chair position (asking her to select her own co-chair from among other candidates you've identified).

USE THEIR TIME WISELY

Ask busy people to lead your effort. But bear in mind that the secret in using the time of busy people is to have them do what is critical to your project and no more.

STAFF STAYS BEHIND THE SCENES

In working with fund raising leadership, staff should perform its function with what one sage calls a "passion for anonymity." Staff members should coordinate, provide technical expertise, clerical support, and whatever resource information might be needed.

Too, staff should do everything in their power to motivate and inspire volunteers.

But always at the center of activity, in the glare of the spotlight, must be the volunteers themselves. You will, in this way, motivate them to assume their full fund raising responsibility.

THERE IS NO SUBSTITUTE

There is no substitute for the influence a leader can have on certain prospective donors (the staff's influence, by comparison, is usually negligible).

And considering that fund raising success is usually dependent on what a limited number of donors do, it becomes paramount that you enlist the right leadership -- "right" meaning that they have the ability to influence the people who will make or break your drive.

Always, always, remember that leadership is *the* key factor in successful fund raising ... no matter the cause, no matter the goal, no matter the scope of your campaign.

3

Making Your Case

To paraphrase the memorable words of Louis "Satchmo" Armstrong, attorneys *do* it. Salesman *do* it. Debaters *do* it. Why, even teenagers *do* it.

They plead their cases, that is, whether it's for second degree manslaughter or the lifting of a curfew on prom night. Everyday, in dozens of different ways, we attempt to motivate others to act. And the more important the action, the more persuasive and sound our reasons must be.

Certainly when you're asking people to part with money, a painful act for the majority of us, you need to supply irrefutable arguments why doing so is beneficial. You need, in other words, to make your case.

Unless you do, and unless the reasons you put forth are credible and convincing, you'll get token support at best. The nine steps described below will enable you to identify, write, and present the strongest case your organization has to offer.

IDENTIFYING YOUR CASE

The simple fact that your organization needs money -- what organization doesn't -- won't lead prospective donors to support you, no matter how well-conceived your campaign.

The questions these prospects want to know are, Why is your organization important, who does it serve, and why does it merit support?

In other words, why should individuals, foundations, and corporations single you out for financial support? What exactly is your case for support?

Answering this requires effort, and the first step is naming a committee to study your long-range objectives -- where your organization is going, how it intends to get there, what resources are needed, and what these resources will allow you to accomplish over the next three to five years.

Only after you've done this, and only after you can express how today's campaign will help you achieve tomorrow's goals, can you create a fund raising program to meet these goals.

This organizational planning process provides the *content* for your case statement, which is, after all, the end product of serious deliberation.

YOUR MISSION IN COMPELLING WORDS

In business parlance, a case statement is your organization's sales pitch. It tells your constituency who you are, what you're trying to accomplish, and why. (Such a statement is important internally as well, in that it helps you, your board, and your volunteers focus sustained attention on your policies and plans).

As clearly and persuasively as possible, your case statement lays out your history, purpose, and plans, but more importantly it presents the reasons why someone should invest in your organization and the benefits that will result from that investment.

People seldom give large gifts to a cause they don't understand, so you will need a compelling and clear case. As mentioned above, the fact that yours is a good cause or that gifts to you are tax deductible isn't motivating to the prospect. People contribute, not to keep doors open, but to help achieve worthwhile objectives.

And the operative word here is people, for your ultimate aim is to convey what the money you seek will do for people rather than your organization.

Fund raising authority Harold Seymour, when summing up the essence of a case statement, put it this way: the case statement "is the one definitive piece of the whole campaign. It tells all that needs to be told, answers all the important questions, reviews the arguments for support, explains the proposed plan for raising the money and shows how gifts may be made, and who the people are who vouch for the project, and who will give it leadership and direction."

WHAT YOUR CASE SHOULD INCLUDE

As your basic fund raising tool, your case, in addition to stating what your organization is and hopes to become, should:

❑ Describe your organization's mission.

❑ Document the need for which you're raising money.

❑ Enunciate your organization's goals, objectives, and long-range plans.

❑ Show your competence to deliver services.

❑ Demonstrate your fiscal stability and the capability of your leadership.

❑ Describe how gifts will be used and the people who will benefit.

❑ Explain how addressing the need will benefit the prospect and the community.

Since there are today a million or so 501(c)(3) organizations in search of philanthropic support, it should be obvious that your organization's case statement serves the vital role of laying the foundation for a successful fund raising drive.

MAKE YOUR CASE DONOR-ORIENTED

Keep in mind, always, that your prospect is infinitely more interested in his or her own personal benefit than in your organization.

Take this book as an example. Why are you reading it? Most likely, you're hoping it will enhance some element of your job. If after a few sentences you decide it's irrelevant, then you'll put it aside and look elsewhere.

The same can be said of prospects reading your case statement. They want to know what's in it for them. You must, therefore, convince them that investing in your organization is a sound thing to do, and that by helping you achieve your goals your prospects are helping themselves and their community. No small task, but essential.

Remember as well that your case should set forth human rather than organizational concerns. What will your organization do for *people*?

As the fund raising axiom goes, people give to people for people. It is these very individuals who will pledge their money, volunteer their time, put your organization into their wills, and influence others to join your effort.

To do all this, your prospect must understand what your organization is doing, why it's doing it, how it affects the prospect, and *how his or her gift will make a difference.*

WHO SHOULD DO THE WRITING?

Since it should represent the thinking of your board and staff, many individuals will likely be involved in formulating your case for support.

In fact, you should consider using a committee to help in the preparation since members can often provide reasons for supporting your mission that you might overlook or take for granted now.

Your organization's leadership -- staff and volunteers -- should review the draft of the statement. This gives both groups a sense of participation, and fosters teamwork, but more importantly it usually makes a difference in the way your inner family accepts the case and embraces the campaign.

As for who should do the actual writing, clearly it should be someone with good prose skills and the capacity to grasp your mission -- one person, not a committee.

While chief executive officers and board members have the responsibility to accept and modify various drafts, it's rare that these people have the talent, time, or inclination to compose the complete case statement.

Of course, if your organization has already conducted several campaigns, you might decide to model your case statement after previous ones. Otherwise you'll need to assess your in-house capabilities or hire a consultant.

HOW TO BEGIN WRITING

Perhaps the best way to begin writing your case statement is to imagine you're addressing the most recalcitrant prospect on earth, someone for whom you'll need to be utterly pragmatic, concise, and to the point.

Jot down the following: The precise reason why your appeal must take place; what you'll achieve if your campaign succeeds, the people who will benefit.

These few sentences will form the core of your case statement.

Once you've drafted a preliminary case, and before proceeding any further, find out if your staff and volunteers are moved by your message. If not, you'll need to begin again.

While it's easier said than done, your finished case statement should be succinct, factual, and donor-centered. It should, with unmistakable clarity, tell prospects what their gifts will do for the things they hold most dear. And it should do so in a way that's completely acceptable to your organization's inner family.

One "formula" for writing an effective case statement is the following:

❑ State the need.
❑ Set forth the arguments why the need must be met.
❑ Anticipate and answer all important questions.
❑ Explain your plans for raising the money.
❑ Show how gifts can be made, and,
❑ Identify the people who will lead the drive.

IS YOUR CASE STATEMENT WELL WRITTEN?

If you can honestly answer "yes" to most, if not all, of the following questions, your case statement is most likely a well-written one.

❑ Does your case hold your reader's attention until the end?
❑ Is it easy to read?
❑ Can your case be read at one sitting?
❑ Is it positive and upbeat?
❑ Is your case donor-centered, that is, does it speak to the prospect's interest rather than yours?
❑ Does it demonstrate the same values as your prospects?
❑ Does your case convey urgency, that action on the prospect's part is required now?
❑ Is what you say supported by facts? And,
❑ Does your case, with uncompromising honesty, reflect your organization and its work?

THE LOOK OF YOUR FINAL PRODUCT

If your appeal is simple and direct, your case statement may be an unassuming two-page letter. On the other hand, if you're erecting a major facility or renovating one, you might need a graphically bold, four-color brochure.

Some case statements are even done as videotapes or slide presentations. Regardless of the format, honesty and unwavering realism are respected.

Content is important, not length (though you'll probably want to be succinct since it will increase the likelihood of your case being read).

Use pictures and charts to illustrate your copy and to make the presentation more interesting.

Avoid overkill. You'll have little luck in trying to persuade prospects of cliches such as your "unique value," your "dedication and loyalty," or your "commitment to high standards."

Finally, avoiding extravagance and high pressure will usually work in your favor.

HOW TO USE IT

There are several effective ways to use your case statement. These include:

1) Having your inner family use the statement -- or, rather, the process of formulating it -- as a means of focusing their thinking on the mission and future of your organization.

2) Sharing a shortened form of the statement with community leaders as part of your market survey (feasibility study).

3) Using the statement as a tool in recruiting leadership.

4) Using the statement to support a customized appeal to a special prospect.

5) Using the statement as the foundation, and reference

source, for all of your publications and communications aimed at supporters.

◆◆◆

In the final analysis, your successful case statement will:

1) Explain your organization's priorities and credibly present your goals and objectives.

2) Make clear that the values of your organization and those of your prospect are shared or similar. And

3) Be dramatic enough to move your organization to the top of your prospects's priority list of charities.

Again, in the words of Harold Seymour, your case will succeed if it "aims high, provides perspective, arouses a sense of history and continuity, conveys a feeling of importance, relevance, and urgency, and has whatever stuff is needed to warm the heart and stir the mind."

4

Prospect Research

As the philanthropy figures from *Giving USA* make clear every year, individuals consistently account for more than 85 percent of the funds contributed annually to charitable organizations.

Countless colleges, health agencies, cultural groups, and social service organizations depend on the support of generous men and women, especially those capable of making major gifts.

It's hardly surprising, then, that thriving development offices make prospect research a priority. Big gifts don't come from strangers, and getting to know people is what research is all about.

If your organization lags in this area, the 12 steps outlined below will acquaint you with a research process that by and large will determine your success or failure in raising substantial money.

WHY IS RESEARCH EVEN NECESSARY?

An often used phrase that still has relevance is that in fund raising the most successful solicitations take place when the right prospect is asked for the right amount by the right solicitor at the right time in the right way.

Enter prospect research, the role of which is to determine, as much as possible, each of these "right" elements. Properly conducted research identifies legitimate prospects, assesses what each can give, pinpoints their interests, and uncovers who's likely to be successful in soliciting them.

An organization secures major gifts when it finds — or creates — a match between its mission and the aspirations of its prospects.

Research is the link in making that match.

WHAT TO DO FIRST

Since there are always more prospects than time to research them, it makes sense to spend the bulk of your time on those with the most potential.

First determine the size of a major gift for your organization and then:

1) Cast a wide net and look for individuals who, experience and common sense tell you, are your best prospects. Who do you serve; whom have you helped; who will need your services in the future; who shares your philosophy? Be inclusive; you can winnow down later.

2) Make a list of all your current and past contributors. If you've been in the development field for long, you know past donors are your best prospects for future gifts.

3) Put together a prospect identification committee. Ordinarily such a group will consist of individuals (bankers, real estate agents, attorneys, CPAs, and business leaders) who are in positions to identify people with money.

YOUR INITIAL FOCUS

Just as when soliciting funds you start at the center and work out, so too with prospect research. You begin with your organization's natural constituents.

First comes your governing board. Maintain an accurate, up-to-date information form on each member.

Next, look to previous donors. As mentioned, those who have given in the past are likely to entertain another request (assuming you've treated them well).

Advisory groups are next, followed by sources such as alumni, former patients, regular attendees, and leaders in your community who have a record of philanthropy.

Beyond these groups, by looking at your own mission you will know where to look for additional prospects.

NARROW THE LIST

Once you have in hand a comprehensive list of potential givers, some preliminary research is required to determine who among them have the means to give a major gift and thus deserve more of your attention.

At this stage, you will generally rely on readily available resources -- both in print and on the Internet -- such as *Standard and Poor's Register, Marquis Who's Who, Forbes 400* list, and of course your own internal records.

The basic information to gather on each suspect is: giving history, name, home and business addresses, business title, nature of business, and family ties to your organization.

This data you will then pass in front of other staff members and volunteers — a screening committee of knowledgeable volunteers is ideal — in order to promote suspects into real prospects.

CAPACITY TO GIVE

With your list of legitimate prospects in hand, you now need to assess each person's ability to give. To do so, examine the following:

• *Salary*

If the person works for a publicly traded company, your

task is fairly easy. You'll find his or her salary — and the remuneration of other upper-level officers — in the company's proxy statement.

If the individual is employed by a privately-owned company, you can (to get a general range) page through a job almanac listing salaries by profession or employment.

• *Stock holdings*

If your prospect is an "inside owner" or five percent owner of a publicly traded company, his or her holdings will be listed in the company's proxy statement.

Too, some companies have on-line services that provide information on inside owners. This service lists the total "direct" and "indirect" stock holdings of each insider owner.

• *Real estate*

It's relatively easy to find out how much a person's home — and other properties — are worth. Simply visit the local assessor's office and review this public information.

• *Inheritance*

Determining inheritance wealth isn't quite as easy. Still, once wills are probated, they are public information and can be examined at the appropriate courthouse.

The enterprising researcher will also review the wills of closely related family members, including the parents of the prospect and the prospect's spouse.

CLARIFYING THE RELATIONSHIP

Once you're confident your prospect has the means to give, the next order of business is defining that person's relationship to you.

Your best source of information (hopefully) can be found within your organization: the records you have on the prospect, notes from past solicitors, and recollections and insights from staff and volunteers.

Principally, you'll be looking to answer such questions as:

How has the prospect been involved with us? Has he or she given in the past? To what programs or projects? The amounts? Have other members of the prospect's family been involved with us?

If your records are spotty, a second way of uncovering links to your organization is to collect it first-hand, by surveying your prospect pool.

While only some will respond, asking your prospects to complete a written survey can provide valuable information about their professional lives, program interests, general feelings toward your organization, even their household income.

INSIGHTS FROM PAST SOLICITORS

If you're lucky enough, probably the best information you can get about a prospect will come from someone who has previously solicited the person.

Assuming the solicitor did his or her homework and was well prepared, he or she should have a clear understanding of the prospect's motivations, interests, and history with your organization.

Who else could offer such a rich source of information but someone who's had direct contact seeking the same thing, namely a contribution?

DEVELOPING FILES

You will of course need a separate file for each of your major gift prospects. The main document in this file, the *prospect information sheet*, should contain the following data:

• Full name, business and home addresses, and telephone numbers.
• Date of birth; place of birth.
• Colleges and graduate schools attended by prospect

and spouse.
- Spouse's name, including wife's maiden name.
- Children's names and birth dates.
- Professional positions held and dates.
- Community activities, including club memberships.
- Political activities.
- Special interests; special honors.
- Estimates of earnings and assets.
- Individuals who know the person well and could provide additional information or solicit a gift.
- Ways in which the individual is connected to the organization.
- Giving history to you and to other organizations.
- Names of attorney and accountant.

It is an ambitious undertaking, gathering all of this data. Still, how else could you hope to understand the prospect and his or her interests in relation to yours?

UPHOLD YOUR INTEGRITY

Seeking background information on a prospect is nothing new. Banks, investment firms, and mortgage companies have done it for years.

The process, when it relies on public sources and information from individuals — and is conducted within ethical policies and guidelines established by the board — is neither wrong nor immoral.

Still, there are privacy issues and you should keep three factors in mind when conducting research.

First, limit your research into a prospect's background to areas relevant to your organizational needs. In other words, don't pursue peripheral information of no concern to you.

Second, be honest and forthright when gathering information. Don't use false names or pretenses.

Third, consider the "embarrassment" factor. Would you,

without reservation, hand over your file to the prospect? If not, you probably have included information that isn't germane to your purposes.

NOT EVERYTHING IS IMPORTANT

Given enough time, and resources, you could compile a foot-high dossier on nearly any prospect. But who would read it?

You want pertinent information only.

For this reason, try to focus your research on four principal questions:

1) How much is the prospect worth?
2) What is he or she *most* interested in?
3) Who has the greatest influence on the prospect?
4) What is our current relationship with him or her?

The goal of research isn't to bury staff and volunteers in an avalanche of data. It is to supply sufficient information that proves useful in developing a solicitation strategy.

WHEN TO STOP GATHERING

Good research, by identifying mutual interests and shared goals between prospects and organizations, makes it "easier" to solicit.

But solicitations are always confrontations of a sort, so there's a tendency for many organizations to continue to research, even after more than enough information has been collected.

Recognize this as a delaying tactic and try to resist it.

You might have conducted superb research, and be armed with mounds of information, but none of it's worth a nickel if you don't get around to closing the sale.

THE FINAL CHECK

If you can answer each of the following questions, you can

be reasonably sure you've researched your prospect well:

1) How much is the individual worth and what form does his or her wealth take?

2) What is the prospect's history of giving to your organization?

3) What is the person's current relationship with your organization?

4) Which of your organizational needs matches the prospect's particular interests?

5) Who are the prospect's peers? And,

6) Among these peers, who has a relationship with your organization and might be willing to solicit the prospect?

While there are important other questions, your ability to answer these six will in good measure demonstrate the quality of your research.

◆◆◆

Often wearisome, sometimes confusing, and more than occasionally frustrating, prospect research is increasingly important in today's donor climate. Successful organizations don't rely on the kindness of strangers. They make a concerted effort to know their constituents, mindful that it is the first step toward securing a major gift.

5

Cultivating Prospects and Donors

As any farmer will attest, seeds sown in untilled soil reap a disappointing crop. The most fruitful harvests come from careful *cultivation* that nourishes the land, preparing it for planting. Thus nurtured, a tended field yields its prolific bounty again and again. And so the word cultivation is an apt description of one of fund raising's proven tenets as well.

At it's heart, raising money is all about building and nurturing relationships. It may take months, it often takes years, to set the stage for a large gift. And there are few, if any shortcuts.

If you want to reap your own share of generous donors, you will find it fruitful to follow the suggestions below.

WHAT CULTIVATION IS

Before prospects will contribute meaningfully, they must know about your organization, its mission and its goals. Asking them to give before they're familiar with you -- to say nothing of committed to you -- is to invite token gifts only.

The goal of an effective cultivation program, therefore, is first to gain your prospects' attention, actively involve them in your work, and *then* offer them the opportunity to give.

For nearly every prospect, you will need to make some cultivation moves, whether through printed materials, special events, or personal attention. And if it's a major gift you're seeking, the more cultivation you'll have to plan.

In fund raising, as experienced staff know, 90 percent is preparation, 10 percent is asking. Cultivation is a major part of that 90 percent.

WHY YOU MUST DO IT

Someone who isn't knowledgeable about your organization isn't going to give you a large gift. Why would they, when they can just as easily contribute to organizations with which they're acquainted?

You must earn major gifts, by introducing prospects to your organization, involving them in your work, and slowly gaining their commitment to your goals.

On one level, good cultivation builds awareness of your organization. But on a deeper level it seeks to build relationships with prospects, to develop a bond between them and your organization.

This explains why it's essential to offer prospects meaningful involvement. You want them to see your organization as an important part of their lives.

To the extent that you develop such strong relationships will determine the degree to which prospects support you.

YOUR GOAL

Your cultivation activities should accomplish at least two important objectives.

The first is to involve the prospect in your organization to the extent that he or she feels a sense of ownership, and wants to aid and abet your work by making a truly substantial gift. The second objective is to instill in the person a habit of giving. Good cultivation isn't aimed at attracting one gift. It is instead an ongoing process of fostering relationships with people to whom you can turn for reliable and generous support.

WHEN TO START

The time to begin involving major prospects in your work is long before you plan any campaign.

This is why it's imperative to establish a cultivation program just as soon as you've identified those individuals -- usually the top 10 percent of your prospects -- who can do you the most good. In fact, these are the very people you want to involve in the planning of your campaign.

Good cultivation is a slow process; ordinarily it will take months, if not years, to cultivate a major gift prospect. On average, it takes anywhere from 18 to 24 months.

For impatient board members, that may seem like a long time. But remember, major gifts often make or break a campaign. It only makes sense to spend ample time cultivating those on whom your success depends.

PROSPECTS TO TARGET

While you want to cast as wide a net as possible when searching for prospects, not every person will be a good candidate for you.

You must perceive that the individual has some interest in your work or, at the very least, you must have some legitimate reason to believe you can plant and nurture the seed of interest.

So as not to waste time, you need to prioritize your prospects, usually into four groups:

- *Group One*

Those ready to give generously if not sacrificially. For these people your organization is near and dear to their heart and they have been involved with you for a period of time.

- *Group Two*

Those who require a small degree of cultivation. They are aware of your work but need to be involved further before they will contribute substantially.

- *Group Three*

Those requiring considerable cultivation. These may include people in the community who support other causes but don't know much if anything about your work.

- *Group Four*

People known to be wealthy but who have no link to your organization, nor as far as you can determine any interest in your kind of work.

You will of course want to focus nearly all of your efforts on the first three groups, perhaps sending some materials, such as your newsletter, to the fourth group in an effort to uncover some interest.

AN ART NOT A SCIENCE

While there are proven techniques of cultivation, still there are no formulas that guarantee success.

How could there be, when the personalities of each of your prospects is unique? What is polite to one may appear impertinent to another.

For this reason, cultivation is more akin to art than to science. You have to be sensitive, tactful, and guided by common sense. But, most importantly, you have to be sincere.

Forget hype and glitzy cultivation programs. They don't work. Instead be yourself, be genuine, and you will have no trouble in attracting supporters to your organization.

IT'S AN ATTITUDE

While cultivation, in essence, is a set of activities building and strengthening relationships with your ~~.ors~~ and prospects, it is first and foremost an attitude. It says, "We value and respect you."

To succeed, you must treat your donors with the same "satisfaction guaranteed" attitude that smart businesses treat customers. They are, after all, as essential to your survival as customers are to a business.

Satisfy your donors and they will return the favor in kind for many years to come.

THE ROLE OF BOARD MEMBERS

Cultivation, especially as it applies to major prospects, is a highly personal matter and board members must be involved.

Board members know who the prospects are, in what circles they move, the nature of their personalities, which activities will be appropriate, and how to reach them.

Further, for some cultivation activities such as escorting prospects to events, seeking their advice, asking them to participate in special projects, or inviting them to serve on committees, overtures by trustees will prove to be far more effective than staff-initiated moves.

CULTIVATION METHODS

Cultivation activities can include anything from sending a newsletter to sending a personal emissary.

In the early stages, when a prospect knows little, if anything, about your organization, factual information in the form of newsletters or special reports can help to build awareness and give the individual a clear sense of your mission.

But to be truly effective, cultivation eventually has to move from the impersonal to the personal.

Activities here range from the prospect helping you to plan a special event, to serving on a special committee, to receiving a personal visit from a trustee or even the president of the organization.

Any and all of these increase the prospect's knowledge of your work and strengthen the bond he or she feels toward you.

While cultivation activities can be elaborate -- think of a testimonial dinner, for instance -- they should include simple gestures too, like asking for advice, asking if you can mention a prospect's name, or if the individual will do you a small favor.

MAKE IT CONTINUOUS

Like you, prospects aren't gullible. They know something's up when you come calling right before the start of a big campaign.

Disingenuous cultivation won't work; it's too manipulative. Instead, you must relate to your prospects and donors at all times, not only when you have a critical need for funds.

As those who are experienced know, cultivation is all about building relationships -- finding common ground, earning trust, and then seeking assistance.

It begins when a person is introduced to your organization; it deepens when he or she gets involved; and it reaches a peak when that individual contributes generously.

Your campaigns may start and end, but your cultivation activities should be ongoing.

MAKE IT NATURAL

Your cultivation initiatives must seem natural to the prospective donor, not contrived. One failsafe and simple way to ensure this is to imagine how you would like to be cultivated.

When planning activities, put yourself in your prospect's shoes and do only those things you feel you would respond to favorably.

BE HONEST

Cultivation isn't a game. It is -- or should be -- a sincere effort to win people over to a cause you yourself believe in.

For this reason, be straightforward about all your activities. Make sure prospects know that the end you're seeking is their trust and financial support.

This isn't to say you need to announce your intention as prospects enter the room; but don't act in a way that misleads your prospects or invites misinterpretation.

There's no better way to create enmity than by pretending to serve one end while really serving another.

AVOID GIMMICKS

Some people are naive when it comes to cultivation.

With some fancy footwork here, a little fawning attention there, to say nothing of an invitation to the ultimate gala, they think they can butter up their prospects and then swoop in for a gift.

But, like you, prospects are too intelligent and perceptive for that sort of treatment. These are influential people, for the most part, who long ago hardened themselves to manipulators. They are not so shallow that superficial attention is going to influence their financial planning.

Consequently, you will only win their support if your cultivation activities are:

1) Honest and straightforward, and
2) Respectful of their time.

Don't think you can "handle" your prospects. They will resist and resent such an approach. Instead, respect them, treat them with dignity, and always be aware of the demands upon their time.

DON'T BE LAVISH

There can be a tendency to overdo when it comes to cultivation activities. After all, your future depends on these prospects and you long to impress them.

But lavishing too much attention and too many things on your prospects tends, on the one hand, to embarrasses them. On the other hand, it can prompt them to question your operation ("These spendthrifts don't need my money").

Be tasteful, be elegant, but don't be extravagant.

◆◆◆

While it takes different forms for different organizations, cultivation is, at heart, still about fostering relationships. To this end, you will be successful, regardless of your type of organization, if you:

❑ Take the time to know your prospects so as to get a feel for the most effective cultivation activities.

❑ Introduce them to aspects within your organization that are in keeping with their interests.

❑ Encourage them to participate in these aspects in a meaningful way, be it serving on a committee or planning a special project.

❑ Communicate regularly, especially when your organization has a new offering that reflects their interest.

❑ Be patient. It normally takes 12 to 18 months to build a strong relationship with a prospective donor.

6

Asking in Person

Personal solicitation. The words cause even the most devoted volunteer to wince. It's difficult, if not impossible, for most of us to ask for money. In fact, the discomfort is so strong we'll find 50 excuses not to get involved (bad weather, aches and pains, a woeful in-law, you name it).

But the inescapable truth is that soliciting a major gift almost always requires a personal visit. Who but Mother Theresa will part with a significant sum without being asked to do so directly?

Alibis aside, making personal calls leads to substantial gifts. That's the plain and unvarnished truth. And, while heeding the suggestions below won't be easy, they will - sooner than you think - lead you down the road to riches.

PUT YOURSELF IN THEIR SHOES

When envisioning a prospect, think of yourself first. Except that they may be wealthier, prospects are the same as everyone else.

They aren't attracted by gimmickry. They're busy people who respond best to direct and concise approaches. Most will react positively to solicitors who are genuinely enthusiastic. They aren't required by any edict to give you money. And few, if any prospects, will make gifts if they aren't asked.

FRIENDS NOT ADVERSARIES

Too many organizations think of fund raising as a "hard sell," even conceiving of their solicitors as a sales force with quotas to meet. How much more appropriate, and effective, to view solicitors as friends to the donor, as counselors trying to help people do something of consequence for the community and for society.

The most successful solicitor isn't overbearing. To the contrary, she listens; she tries to find out what's on the mind of the prospect.

Her job isn't to coerce, or to convince others of what they *should* do. Rather, it is to listen and to relate the aims of her organization to what people already want.

In other words, a successful solicitation is always donor-centered, providing satisfaction and fulfillment to the giver rather than programming him to accept what your organization has to offer.

SAVE THE SOLICITING FOR LAST

How do you obtain money for a cause? Simple, a neophyte might say. Find rich people and ask them to give it. Well, not exactly.

Granted, the prospect must have means, but, as important, he must have motivation. And that, as veterans know, comes from involving him in your organization, sharing your goals in an honest and heartfelt way, and otherwise cultivating the person - often over a period of years - to make a substantial investment in your organization.

In other words, soliciting is the final, not the first, step in the fund raising process.

To grasp this, keep in mind the four categories of prospects:

1) Those ready to make a substantial gift.

2) Those needing some cultivation before they'll consider a significant gift.

3) Those needing extensive cultivation. And,

4) Those with the capacity to give but with no reason to do so.

GIVE BEFORE GETTING

As Socrates said, "Let him that would move the world first move himself." In fund raising, this means solicitors must give before asking others to do so. Nothing is more persuasive with prospective donors.

When a solicitor embarks without having contributed, not only does she solicit with less conviction, and less enthusiasm, but she's vulnerable to the legitimate charge, "Why should I, a prospect, give if you, who are closer to the organization, haven't?"

Early and generous giving by your organization's leaders demonstrates a commitment and gives the campaign its impetus. Failure at this level can, and usually does, jeopardize the success of the entire effort.

TECHNIQUE DOES MATTER

You may have scores of volunteers committed to your cause, but few if any have real experience in asking others to give. They will find it easy to talk about your programs and your achievements, but they won't know how to ask for a contribution. You must therefore train these individuals in a few simple techniques: how to get the appointment, make the case, ask for the gift, and close.

Don't mistakenly assume that some of your volunteers know how to ask for a gift, even when they've been involved in previous campaigns.

Quite often the contrary is true. They may have called upon prospects in previous drives, true. But the gift they secured may not have been as significant as it could have been with a better presentation.

KNOW YOUR PROSPECT

The more your solicitor knows about the prospect, the greater the likelihood of securing a gift.

Solicitors should receive a profile of each major prospect, including pertinent biographical data, a record of gifts to your organization, other services to your organization, important contributions to other causes, special philanthropic and personal interests, and social affiliations.

MATCHMAKING IS KEY

A solicitor who makes a $100 commitment to your cause should call on prospects who are capable of giving a similar amount. Likewise, a $500 prospect is best approached by a solicitor who himself has contributed a similar sum.

But as important as matching like amounts is pinpointing just the right solicitor. Some prospects expect to be asked by the president or the chairman of the board. Others are less formal and would welcome the person they know best from the organization to ask for the gift. Still others may need the ego-stroking of a team of solicitors.

Reading this dynamic correctly is *the* key to success. As the old saw goes, people give to the person who asks, not to the organization.

FAST OUT OF THE GATE

People who contribute first set the pace for those who follow. It pays therefore to devote close attention to the order in which you approach your prospects.

For example, if your first contribution comes in at $5,000, rather than the $2,500 you expected, your next prospect, challenged by the loftier sum, might well give $2,000 rather than the $1,000 she was considering. This kind of ripple effect can carry through the campaign.

Of course, it can work in reverse too. If your first contribution is a $1,000 check, instead of the hoped-for $2,500, then the next prospect might scale back his anticipated $1,000 contribution to only $500.

DON'T OVERWORK SOLICITORS

While recommendations vary, one solicitor personally calling upon five prospects is a fairly standard measure for major gift campaigns. Asking solicitors to do more usually results in procrastination and may lead to telephone or mail contacts rather than personal visits.

DREAM TEAMS

It's almost always a good idea to solicit major gifts in 'teams. Team members -- two, three, or even four of them -- not only reinforce one another, they're usually better equipped to answer questions and raise salient points. Some effective teams include:

1) Volunteer and chief executive officer
2) Volunteer and staff member
3) Chief executive officer and staff member

When using the team approach, be sure all participants are working on the same solicitation plan and have identical objectives in mind.

ONCE IS NOT ENOUGH

Before a substantial gift can be secured, a solicitor may have to call on the prospect two, three, or even four times. In fact, it's not unusual to use the initial visit simply to provide information, answer questions, and serve as a sort of "community investment" counselor.

Some, like fund raising expert Si Seymour, go so far as to say that if a major prospect pledges during the first visit, the solicitor has failed to ask for enough (more gestation time would have been needed for a truly sacrificial pledge).

Don't rush a prospect into a premature "no" or a token gift. Better to give her time to think it over and yourself time to rethink your approach.

GET THE APPOINTMENT BUT BE DISCREET

When should the phone be used in personal solicitation? Almost never.

The one exception, of course, is to set up an appointment with the prospect (and great care must be taken here not to discuss the gift sought).

If the prospect insists upon knowing the nature of the visit, the solicitor can simply say he has a favor to ask and would prefer to do it personally.

INTRODUCE A LITTLE ROMANCE

Just the facts ma'am may have worked for Jack Webb, but cold facts alone don't motivate donors and prospects. A little romance does.

When presenting your case, weave a vivid tapestry for the prospect. The challenges you've overcome, the founders who dreamed, the workers who sacrificed, the girls, boys, women, and men whose lives have been changed - put your emphasis here.

Present the facts, yes, but add the sweetener of romance. Learn from Charles Revson, founder of Revlon, who said, "We don't manufacture cosmetics, we sell hope."

HOLD YOUR TONGUE

Silence has a role in a successful solicitation. In fact, the person who won't stop talking is the most unconvincing solicitor in the world.

Silence not only gives the prospect a turn, it also puts everything squarely on her shoulders. She has to respond now, if only to raise objections that you must address.

Fight the natural urge to fill in uncomfortable silences and your chances of success will increase.

ASK FOR THE GIFT ... AND BE SPECIFIC.

Never ask for money until you've sold your project, but don't leave the prospect without asking for the "order" either. Despite your best research, and your sustained effort to cultivate and involve the prospect, it's all for naught if you don't ask.

And be specific!

Most prospective donors want guidance - the more specific the better. Asking for "Whatever you can do" is a prescription for failure (it also implies you're ambiguous about your goals). By requesting a specific amount - "we *hope* you will give $500" - you show you've given careful thought to the campaign and you put the prospect in a position of having to respond. The suggested amount becomes a frame of reference, one that will get serious consideration if the solicitor is a friend or peer.

RESPONDING TO OBJECTIONS

During most solicitations, the prospect will invariably raise objections. Who wouldn't, if they were being asked for a substantial sum of money?

Whatever the objection, and regardless of its merit, don't reply in haste (as if you're either defensive or programmed). Instead, ponder a moment, then give a courteous, informed answer. Objections are really questions, after all, and by answering them you move the prospect closer to giving.

If despite your best effort, a "no" seems impending, leave without closing and set a date for a possible follow-up meeting. This will give you time to plan a new strategy taking into account what you've learned.

ONE SIZE DOESN'T FIT ALL

Most donors will give more if they know they can spread their gift over a period of years.

By being flexible, and offering donors a combination of devices, you'll encourage greater generosity. Make available installment pledges; accept gifts of appreciated securities, trusts, real estate, and insurance; and consider a program of named commemorative opportunities.

BE OFF

Conclude the visit with your prospect as soon as the pledge is signed or the gift received. Otherwise, like a rookie salesperson, you could "unsell" the customer with a verbal miscue.

Since the purpose of your call is fulfilled when the commitment is made, you should thank the donor and leave immediately.

DON'T LEAVE A PLEDGE CARD

It's better not to leave a pledge card with the prospect, although some swear by it. If the card is left, the solicitor loses a primary reason to follow up, and it's possible the prospect will either file it or make an insubstantial gift.

◆◆◆

When all is said and done, solicitors inherently know the best technique for soliciting gifts. All they need to do, as John D. Rockefeller put it many years ago, is ask themselves one question, "How would I like to be approached for a gift?" The answer, if carefully thought out, "may be relied upon as a pretty safe guide to the task of soliciting."

The essentials Rockefeller laid out for a successful solicitation are as accurate today as the day they were penned.

1) The cause must be worthy, and you, the solicitor, must be informed.

2) You should know as much as possible about the person you are calling on.

3) You should give this person an idea as to the contributions others in his or her group are making.

4) You should suggest what you might like the prospect to give, leaving it to him or her to make the final decision. And

5) You should be kindly and considerate: "Thus you will get closest to a man's heart and his pocketbook."

7

Securing Major Gifts

Major gifts are all the rage these days -- and well they should be. In the past 25 years, the rich have indeed gotten richer. Today, five percent of us earn an average of more than $250,000 per year. The *really* fortunate few -- the top one percent -- bring home close to a cool million.

Compare these earnings to the median income of a middle-class family -- about $45,000 -- and it's easy to see why most every organization today targets the well-to-do.

With interest in major gifts running high, there are a plethora of books on the subject. Some are superb, others mediocre. But what they all have in common, and what they are all premised upon, is a host of essential tenets.

If you hope to identify, cultivate, and successfully solicit the affluent, you must fully understand the following.

MAKE SURE YOU'RE READY

To determine your overall readiness for a major gifts drive, you'll have to candidly answer some tough questions:

❑ Does your organization really know itself?

❑ Do you have a history of philanthropic support?

❑ Is your organization seen as a positive asset to the

community?

❑ Do board members and staff agree the cause is worthwhile? Will they give time and funds?

❑ Is your case for support compelling?

❑ Do you have the leadership to undertake a major gifts drive?

❑ Do you have an active prospect cultivation program?

❑ Can you identify more than a handful of major gift prospects and a loyal giving constituency below that level?

If you can't answer "yes" to all of these questions, you're probably not ready.

LOOK TO THOSE INVOLVED

Contrary to many a board member's wish, big gifts rarely come from strangers. They come from insiders -- board members and other close friends with a deep commitment to your organization.

The more people know about you and the more involved they are, the more likely they are to be committed to your objectives.

YOUR BEST PROSPECTS ALREADY GIVE

To succeed in raising big gifts, you must have an active fund raising program already in place. Which is to say, without a constituency that's already cultivated and giving, you're destined to fail.

It's rare that donors will make a truly big gift without any prior experience of giving or history with your organization. To the contrary, those who are likeliest to make a significant gift have given to you in the past.

Look at your annual fund donors. Who consistently makes gifts higher than the average? Who increases their gifts each time you ask? These are your prime prospects for increased giving.

CULTIVATION IS EVERYTHING

How important is donor cultivation? Well, some large institutions have "principal" gift directors whose primary job it is to plan and orchestrate the step-by-step involvement of major donor prospects.

In other words, soliciting an extraordinary gift is often a painstaking process.

It's not unusual to spend 98 percent of the time cultivating, and only two percent directed toward the actual ask. In fact, the ask itself is the culmination of a series of cultivation steps. By that time, the prospect will often *want* to do something that's already become attractive to him or her.

MIXED MOTIVATIONS PREVAIL

While motivations like guilt, obligation, fear, and power are usually cited, the simple fact is that no single factor predominates when a donor makes a major gift. More likely, what's involved is a combination of feelings, timing, past giving habits, and the urgency of the moment.

One single fact does stand out, however. Passion, rather than reason, rules. How many people make a list of the institutions seeking their support and then coolly weigh the pros and cons of each? Not many. Most people follow their emotions, a sort of, I love this place, and what they are trying to do. These people inspire and excite me.

TAX REASONS AREN'T PRIMARY

A donor's tax benefits are the same no matter which organization he or she supports; so selling tax benefits isn't the best way to sell your own distinctive cause.

In fact, you're better off assuming tax concerns won't have any impact.

Granted, tax advantages matter and may even dictate when a gift is made. But commitment and interest in your cause spark the gift, so place the full strength and power of your presentation on the mission of your institution, not on the IRS.

SINKING SHIPS SINK

Donors buy dreams and visions; they don't open their hearts, much less their wallets, to strapped organizations needing to be bailed out. The age-old human tendency, joining a successful bandwagon, applies full force.

For major donors, there's little comfort in making a big gift unless the organization has demonstrated fiscal soundness in the past and shows the same for the future.

YOUR ORGANIZATION PREVAILS

While you may have an appealing project to offer, big donors are interested, first and foremost, in your organization. They must have an unswerving belief in your objectives and mission before they'll open their checkbooks.

That's why, to be successful, you must first sell the organization with all the ardor you can muster. Only afterward is it time to describe your specific project and how it will benefit mankind.

TRIED AND TRUE

If you want a major gift for an experimental or unpopular cause, a foundation is your source, not an individual. Very few major donors give to unconventional causes.

This isn't to say they like staid projects. To the contrary, big donors like audacious plans, ones that expand horizons. But they do prefer having dreams spun by established organizations.

STAFF LEADERSHIP IS CRUCIAL

Big givers respond to strong and capable staff leadership.

In fact, the staff leadership of an organization is one of the core factors in motivating a gift. If for any reason donors are turned off or don't have a high regard and respect for those running the show, especially the chief executive officer, they won't give. Big gifts are invariably made to institutions where there's a secure bond of respect and trust between the donor and the institution's chief staff person.

PEER TO PEER MAY NOT BE THE ANSWER

It's axiomatic in fund raising that the best solicitation occurs when the right prospect is asked by the right solicitor. But who is the best solicitor? A volunteer, a staff member, a friend, or a combination thereof?

Despite what many say, there are no hard and fast rules. It depends on each organization's circumstances.

What is clear, however, according to Jerold Panas who queried dozens of million dollar donors for his book *Mega Gifts*, is that the chief executive officer of an institution is the single most important and effective representative.

As for who might accompany the CEO, Panas debunks the myth that no more than two people should call upon a prospect. Take as many people as needed, he counsels -- no fewer, no more (assuming you've given careful thought to each person's role).

GET THE APPOINTMENT

While peer-to-peer soliciting may be less important than many believe, where a peer relationship is critical is in making the appointment. For it is often more difficult to get to see the major prospect than it is to get the gift. Get a peer to make the appointment and have them go along on the call.

DON'T DO LUNCH

A restaurant setting, with its many distractions ("more

coffee, ma'am," "any dessert?") measurably takes away from the focus and objective of your meeting with the major gift prospect.

Better to avoid meetings over meals or in public places and suggest a place where you think the prospect will be most comfortable and fewer distractions will occur.

MATERIALS HOLD LITTLE SWAY

Most organizations start with campaign literature, very often four-color brochures with heart-wrenching themes. But this type of selling with major prospects is often ineffective. Better to proceed as simply and as personally as possible.

Rather than show your organization on paper, talk about it; its special mission, the unmet need it serves, and how your project can meet both the objectives of your organization and the wishes of the donor.

Campaign literature validates your program and has its place. But it should be used to support - not supplant - a verbal presentation.

Whereas details and specifics seldom move big donors, simple talking -- and listening -- often do.

YOU MUST ASK

The cardinal rule of sales is, Make sure you ask for the order.

The same applies to soliciting major gifts.

It's a truism in fund raising that a cause will be hurt more by those who would have said yes but were not asked, than by those who say no.

Too often this principle is overlooked. The solicitor makes a superb case, aided by flawless materials, but when push comes to shove and the time is ripe to ask, the mouth fills with cotton.

Gulp it down or no gift will be forthcoming.

BE RELUCTANT TO ACCEPT A SMALL GIFT

Asking provokes anxiety; so some solicitors are so relieved when they've voiced their request that they'll take any gift, even if the $50,000 prospect offers $5,000.

However, if the prospect's first offer is too low, solicitors should be careful not to accept it. The role of the solicitor is something of a negotiator, to guide and gauge the prospect's increasing interest, to determine the highest possible level, and, finally, to ask for that support.

If a low amount is offered, the solicitor should again stress the importance of the project and describe how he or she has given at a sacrificial level for this very reason. If all else fails, consider resuming the conversation at a future date when a different approach has been plotted.

ONCE IS NOT ENOUGH

It's almost certain that, to get a gift at the level you seek, you will have to make several calls upon the prospect.

In fact, it's best to assume you won't receive a meaningful answer or a significant gift during your first visit. (If you think you have, you're almost always wrong and odds are you could have gotten more!)

Selling the drama, the power, and the excitement of your organization - that's the charge at your first meeting. A later meeting will produce the gift.

A DONOR'S LARGE GIFT WON'T BE HIS LAST.

Major donors don't flip-flop, that is, they don't bounce back and forth from one program and one organization to another. They tend to stay with those causes which have been of interest to them over a long period of time.

For them, giving becomes a habit. As a result, rarely will a large gift be the donor's last. It'll usually be followed by others of ever-increasing size.

RECOGNITION IS WELCOMED

While they may not ask for or seek it, appropriate recognition is welcomed and appreciated by major donors. However, it is up to the staff person to initiate the idea, encourage it, and review it with the donor. The dividends will be immense, especially as sincerely expressed gratitude is the first step in securing another and larger gift.

◆◆◆

When all is said and done, winning big gifts is quite simple. All you need do of a prospect, as Si Seymour put it years ago, is "catch the eye, warm the heart, and stir the mind."

The money will flow.

8

Successful
Special Events

They come in all shapes and sizes: small, big, tiny, colossal. They raise hundreds of dollars; they raise millions. They're elaborate affairs; they're elegantly simple.

They attract legions; they're for an intimate few.

They are, in short, special events, perhaps the most prevalent type of fund raiser around.

But despite their individual character and nuances, successful events all share this in common - they must be smartly conceived, expertly planned, and executed with precision.

By following the recommendations outlined below, you should be well on your way to accomplishing that trio of objectives.

CORE REQUIREMENTS

To be considered truly successful, special events should meet certain requirements, the most important of which are the following:

1) They raise a substantial amount of money.

2) Your committee members - prior to the event - sell

tickets face-to-face.

3) You target your event to people who can afford it and are willing to support you by attending.

4) Your event promotes continuing support for your organization, through a sustained effort to follow-up with individuals introduced to you through the event.

5) You plan and execute your event well, down to the last nut and bolt.

MONEY ISN'T YOUR ONLY OBJECTIVE

A successful event, in addition to raising money, can produce other favorable outcomes.

For instance, there are "soft" objectives like boosting morale throughout your organization, fostering friendships among your trustees and volunteers, and having a lot of fun. Then, too, there are more substantive objectives. These include:

❑ Building productive relationships with corporate sponsors.

❑ Attracting new leaders with potential for the future.

❑ Identifying new donors.

❑ Even permanently upgrading the giving level of many of your current donors.

BEFORE TAKING THE LEAP

When it comes to special events, there's a simple question to ask at the outset: How likely are we to make money if we hold this event?

It's surprising how many volunteers and staff go to lengths to avoid this elementary question.

Then again, maybe it's not surprising since many events are born out of sheer impulse. Money is needed or there's an unexpected shortfall and someone says, "Let's have a dinner dance," or a walk-a-thon, or a craft fair. In the blink of an eye, the idea is adopted, frantic activity ensues, and at the end everyone is exhausted. And, oh yes, not that much money was raised but, well, that's the way it goes.

Not necessarily. A wiser course is to have a cool head, exercise a little discipline, and ask these questions:

❑ What is a realistic goal for this event?

❑ What expenses will we incur?

❑ Do we have sufficient volunteers?

❑ How much time will be required on the part of our staff?

❑ Will the event conflict with other annual fund activities?

❑ Is there enough interest and means in the community to make this event work?

❑ Will we be competing against similar events at the same time?

❑ Will this event add to or detract from our image in the community?

BEWARE OF WARNING SIGNS

While you and your volunteers might be gung-ho about holding the biggest Fantasy Ball Sheboygan has ever seen, if your answer is "no" or "not sure" to any of the following questions it could well be time to temper your enthusiasm:

❑ Have you identified a potential chairperson who is both qualified and willing to work?

❑ Are your volunteers -- assuming you have a multitude of them -- organized and ready to help?

❑ Do you have a dedicated board?

❑ Is there sufficient lead time to plan the event?

❑ Can your staff, or a staff member, devote ample attention to it?

❑ Can you pinpoint enough potential sponsors and ticket buyers to make a substantial profit?

If, with inscrutable honesty you can answer each of these questions in the affirmative, you are indeed ready to proceed.

WILL YOU NEED A CONSULTANT?

An event consultant, you should be aware, doesn't do your work for you. You are still in charge. You are the one, for example, still responsible for recruiting a corps of volunteers.

Nor will a reputable consultant promise that you'll make your goal. It is, after all, still your committee's responsibility to find underwriting and sell tickets.

Still, a veteran consultant can save you time and money. He or she knows from experience what works and what doesn't, and, if brought in early, can steer your volunteers away from wildly ambitious or unrealistic ideas. Too, a consultant, unlike a harried staff member, can give your event undivided attention.

Finally, an experienced event consultant is often adept at negotiating the best prices for catering, printing, and entertainment since he or she usually has ongoing relationships with such providers.

LEADERSHIP

It goes without saying that people are the essential element in making any event happen. And the most instrumental person is a capable chairperson, one who is dependable, works hard, and not only attracts good committee workers but draws out their best effort.

Your chairperson's responsibilities fall into two principal areas: those dealing with finances and those dealing with people.

With regard to finances, your chairperson must develop and adhere to a budget, locate underwriting, keep taps on expenses and ticket sales, and present a final report detailing expenses and net profit.

With respect to underwriting -- of paramount importance if you're to realize a high net -- it helps greatly if your chairperson knows businesspeople and wealthy individuals in a position to make financial decisions. It further helps if he or she has no compunction about calling upon these people for their support.

Your chairperson's other prime responsibility is to recruit and manage a large volunteer force. The ideal chairperson will therefore have a wide network of contacts, including people in business, politics, and various professions.

One final aside: avoid choosing an event and then attempting to find a chairperson. You'll have a much more enthusiastic leader if he or she plays a meaningful role in selecting and shaping the event. It will then be his or her vision to realize.

THE BIGGER THE COMMITTEE, THE BETTER

Generally speaking, the more people you can meaningfully involve on committees, the more successful your event.

Granted, that's unusual, for committees often make progress in inverse proportion to the number of persons sitting on them. But with special events, a different dynamic seems in force. For one thing, fence-sitters, and more than a few prominent people, wait to see who else is involved before joining. And an impressive committee is often enough to entice them.

A second reason for having a large committee is that every member is expected to buy a pair of tickets. A number of your volunteers will bristle at this, feeling their time and effort should count as their contributions. But giving away tickets cuts into your profits and in effect undermines the work your volunteers are putting in.

It's not necessary, of course, to have a mammoth committee in place before you begin. Rather, get started immediately with your new recruits and their initial enthusiasm will inevitably attract additional volunteers.

CHOOSING THE EVENT

When choosing a special event, several factors should be considered: Is the event appropriate? What image will it convey? How much volunteer effort is required? How much front money is needed? Can the event be repeated? And how does the event fit into your overall fund raising program?

• *Appropriateness*

Deciding whether an event is appropriate is relatively simple. Ask yourself, "If the only thing people knew about us was that we sponsored this event, what would their opinion be?" The event is usually appropriate if the answer is either neutral or good.

• *Volunteer effort*

How many volunteers are needed to orchestrate this event, not only for the planning but also to be on hand to coordinate all the details on event day. Do you have that many people available to you?

• *Money up front*

Front money is required for most special events, the grander the event the larger the sum. Whatever the amount -- be it hundreds or thousands of dollars -- this is money you must be able to lose if your event is cancelled.

• *Repeatability*

The best event is a repeatable one, that is, your road race or gala or swim-a-thon builds each year and becomes an event people look forward to. Keep this repeatability factor in mind when selecting your event and don't discard your event simply because the turnout is small the first go-around.

• *The fit with overall fund raising*

Of course, when choosing an event, you'll also want to keep in mind its impact on operating funds -- particularly if your event is profitable. Say you conduct a successful auction and net $75,000 for current operations. How will you raise this money next year? Can you hold another auction? Is it likely be as successful? And will you or your volunteers even want to do it again?

If your event can't be repeated each year with equal success, you must be prepared to increase your annual campaign goal and raise the money elsewhere.

HOW LARGE A DOLLAR GOAL?

While your organization's need will influence the dollar goal you set, more than anything your goal should be dictated by a realistic assessment of your board's resources and how influential your event committee is.

Therefore, when establishing a dollar goal, ask yourself the following questions:

❏ Are our board members active and aware of their financial obligations?

❏ Are they influential, that is, do they have contacts in business and politics?

❏ How much do they give annually and, realistically speaking, can they afford to give more?

To the extent you can answer "yes" to these questions, your goal can be larger, as you can probably rely on your board members to come to the event and bring their friends, help you secure underwriting, and attract guests who will add pizzazz.

BUDGETING

The cardinal rule for any successful event is ... income must exceed expenses. Granted, that's obvious, but it's something difficult to achieve. Which is why a well-constructed budget is indispensable. A budget:

• *Forces you to think through your whole event in*

advance.

When you begin comparing estimated expenses with revenue, you may well discover your whole idea is unworkable and move on to some other event. At the very least, you'll be forced to adjust the numbers so as not to take a financial bath.

- *Helps you keep expenses in line.*

Once you've put on paper the amount you have to work with, you'll think twice about exceeding that sum, whether it's overspending on decorations, cost per plate, or entertainment.

- *Establishes accountability.*

With a budget in hand, every subcommittee chair will know how his or her area of responsibility fits into the overall financial scheme.

- *Helps you identify items that can be underwritten.*

Generally speaking, corporate sponsors prefer to underwrite a specific line item, rather than contribute to general expenses. By listing your expenses, you'll identify items at various price levels that could be proposed to underwriters.

- *Encourages you to work harder.*

Once you've put your projections on paper, a funny thing happens: you feel more committed to realizing them. Say your ticket sales, six weeks before the event, begin to lag. Odds are, you'll redouble your efforts to make your projections.

- *Demonstrates to your board and potential underwriters that you're well organized.*

Most of your board members, and virtually all of your underwriting prospects, work with numbers. By preparing a budget, and demonstrating your financial prowess, you'll more easily gain their critical support.

SEEKING CORPORATE SPONSORS

To undergird the finances of your event, and to maximize proceeds from ticket sales, you'll often find it advantageous to find a corporate sponsor.

In some cases, such a sponsor may cover all of your big expenses, but more often the company will pay for a specific line item, or contribute gifts in kind such as design and printing.

When seeking a corporate partner, personal contact is always favored, especially if your request is substantial. Go as high up the ladder as you can, preferably to the owner or CEO. The person who knows the prospect best should call for the appointment.

If no one in your group has a personal relationship with the prospect, then your top board member should make the approach. If it seems appropriate, a team consisting of the board president, event chair, and executive director might make the visit.

If you're asked to submit a written proposal, keep it simple -- one or two pages on your organization's letterhead describing the event and explaining why you think the company will benefit from being a sponsor. Itemize your financial needs. Then enclose a brochure or annual report detailing your mission and activities, a list of trustees, and a budget for the current fiscal year showing how proceeds from the event are used.

The bottom line is this: corporations sponsor events because it makes business sense. If you package your request so that it clearly spells out the benefits the company will receive, you'll have a decided edge in attracting the sponsor you want.

A final word: the best time to approach a potential

underwriter is as soon as you've developed a concept, not when you're in the throes of the event.

HOW TO PRICE TICKETS

Just how much you charge for tickets depends on several factors: research, judgment, and tempered optimism.

Begin by looking at the giving patterns of your own constituency. Are they accustomed to giving generously and dependably to you, whether it's for your annual drive, capital campaign, or special project? If they are, you can usually set higher ticket prices than otherwise.

But if your current donors aren't in the *habit* of giving, you'll have to ask yourself if that's because they can't afford to or because they haven't been asked in the right way. You'll need an answer to this, so as not to set prices too high.

Consider these six questions when you price your tickets:

❑ How much money do we want to raise from this event?

❑ What do others usually charge?

❑ Are there "hidden" costs to attend (such as paying a babysitter, or parking, or drinks)?

❑ Can we depend on other income (such as an auction or raffle)?

❑ Can we have multi-level ticket pricing?

❑ Will the cost of the ticket affect our image?

A final note: If you've never held this type of event before, don't assume people will pay as much for your inaugural effort as they will for an event with tradition. Often they won't.

GETTING PUBLICITY

Most of your publicity efforts will be directed toward the local media since they reach the people most likely to attend or to be involved as volunteers.

Therefore, look for the local angle. A straight press release about your event may be tossed, but when it also explains how the biggest company in town is sponsoring the event -- to the tune of $25,000 -- then the story becomes newsworthy.

Also, rather than describe how the proceeds of your event will help build a new school, focus on how that school will benefit the community. In other words, stress the human element (the kids), not the inanimate (the building).

Remember too to send invitations to local society editors. They're usually interested in committee members who are notable and will often attend your event. But be ready to help them buttonhole these prominent folks for interviews, comments, or photos.

Finally, you can dramatically increase your chances for local TV coverage when you involve news anchors or reporters in your planning or you invite them to participate in highly visual event activities. Further, if yours is a large public event, invite a local radio station to broadcast from the site. It'll be excellent publicity for you, and good advertising for the station.

WORKING WITH SUPPLIERS

In order to work efficiently with suppliers, be they caterers, florists, printers, or designers, keep the following points in mind:

- *Assign one or two people to work with the supplier.*

No supplier wants to receive phone calls from a handful of people every day, all with different suggestions.

- *Be honest about your budget.*

On day one, tell your supplier how much you can spend and he'll show you what you can accomplish with that amount.

- *Be prepared.*

Say, for example, you've identified a printer. Bring to your meeting some examples of the types of materials you'll need printed.

- *Be reasonable.*

If you expect the supplier to stay within your budget don't demand, for example, the most costly paper or floral arrangements. Be willing to compromise and accept a notch or two down from the best.

- *Trust your supplier.*

Hire someone you're comfortable with and then listen to his suggestions. He's a professional and your second-guessing won't work in your favor.

SWEAT THE DETAILS

With most events, you will need...

- ❑ Adequate insurance
- ❑ Receipts
- ❑ Cash boxes with proper denominations for each box
- ❑ Police and fire numbers in the event of an emergency
- ❑ First aid kit
- ❑ Pens, tape, poster board, and markers
- ❑ Phone numbers of key participants
- ❑ Fire extinguisher
- ❑ Sound system in working order
- ❑ Liquor license
- ❑ Transportation (not only of food and drink, but of any speakers and performers)
- ❑ Lodging for selected participants
- ❑ Parking
- ❑ Plates, utensils, and napkins if there is food

You may also need to consider child care, provisions for the hearing impaired (sign language translation), and wheelchair accessibility.

EVALUATING YOUR EVENT

Once your event is over, it's evaluation time. By asking the following questions, you'll prepare yourself to make next year's event even more profitable.

❑ Did those who attended the event enjoy it?

❑ Did they feel welcomed?

❑ How did they feel about our organization before the event? And afterward?

❑ Did attendees like the location?

❑ Was the food enjoyable?

❑ What part of the event was most important?

❑ What part was unnecessary?

❑ Did people feel they got their money's worth?

❑ Would these same people attend the event next year?

❑ How was the timing of the event (a good time of year, month, week, day)?

❑ Do you think attendees would recommend this event to their friends?

❑ In general, how might we improve the event next time?

THANKING

Despite all the plaques, certificates, and tie-pins, the simplest and most effective thank-you is still a handwritten note. No matter how expensive, a gift can't really substitute for this simple show of gratitude.

9

Direct Mail: Is it for You?

Volumes could be -- and have been -- written about the subject of direct mail as it applies to fund raising. The intent of this chapter is to outline the essential components of direct mail and offer a sampling of "do's and don'ts" generally adhered to by those who consistently succeed with direct mail.

As you read this overview, bear in mind direct mail is both an art and a science and that for every rule there is, alas, an exception.

SHOULD YOU MAIL?

Your organization's potential for success depends on how many of the following questions you can respond affirmatively to. The larger the number, the likelier you are to succeed.

1) Do you have name recognition locally, regionally or nationally?

2) Do you deal with concrete issues rather than abstract ideas?

3) Do you aid specific groups such as the elderly, children, minorities, the disadvantaged or the poor?

4) Is your agency, or the service it provides, unique in some way?

5) Do you have a track record?

6) Is there an issue, a crisis, or an emergency your agency can dramatize?

7) If your mailing fails to recoup half of its cost, will you be able to survive financially?

WHO ARE YOUR PROSPECTS?

Some mail appeals raise significant sums, others don't even recoup their postage costs. While there are a multitude of reasons for success and failure, perhaps *the* most important requirement for success is knowing your market -- knowing to whom you're writing and what makes them tick.

Your potential donor market will be found among three types of lists:

• *Donor lists*

Either your donors or donors to organizations whose missions are similar to yours.

• *Commercial lists*

Magazine subscribers, catalog buyers, credit card holders, Mercedes owners -- the categories are endless.

• *Compiled lists*

Names and addresses culled from telephone books, directories, voting lists, and other public records.

For nonprofit organizations, the types of lists that generally work best are donor lists, followed by carefully selected commercial lists. Compiled lists are the least profitable.

You can rent lists either from a list broker or another organization (most brokers will send you a free catalog of the lists they have available). The costs range from $50 per thousand names and up.

WITH PEN IN HAND

Probably the single most important word a writer can use when drafting a fund raising appeal is "you." The second person singular can rarely be overused. Regrettably, many organizations talk in terms of "our" needs and "our" wants and neglect to convey why the reader should get involved, and how and why "you" will benefit.

To motivate someone to give, you must make your project personal. You must communicate what the gift will mean for the donor, for his family, his community, his society.

Once you're able to strike this tone, keep the following tips in mind:

1) Don't use a fancy font. Instead, use Courier or something similar.

2) Don't omit the saluation, even if it's *Dear Friend*. And, to look more authentic, put a date on your letter.

3) Avoid long paragraphs or a series of short ones. In other words, vary the look of the copy.

4) Underlining, indenting, checkmarks, margin notes -- these are all effective so long as you don't overdo them.

5) Imagine you're writing to one person.

6) Don't bury your request for money. Ask early and ask for a specific amount. Donors like guideposts.

7) Have only one person sign your letter. It's less personal otherwise.

8) Use a P.S. to call for action. Studies indicate a person often reads the postscript before reading the letter.

9) Avoid jargon, long words and technical terms. They reduce readability.

A LONG OR SHORT LETTER?

You'd never read a four-page fund raising letter, you say? You may not be typical.

According to some studies, about 80 percent of the time a two-page letter outpulls a single-page letter. And about 50 percent of the time a four-page letter outpulls a two-page letter.

People don't have time to read long letters?

Bear in mind that if a long letter is compelling, and is attractively laid out and illustrated, you can command the reader's attention for just as long as any newspaper or magazine article can. Also, remember, if a prospective donor is initially interested in your subject, he or she will want to know more.

In general, the more popular and publicized your cause, the shorter your letter can be. Organizations with "brand" names like Easter Seal and American Red Cross can successfully use simple message slips, whereas Save the Irisis of Ypsilanti probably cannot.

THE LETTER IS WRITTEN, ARE YOU DONE?

Composing the letter is just one element of direct mail fund raising. Unless properly "packaged," your letter may not fulfill its purpose, namely, attracting attention, stimulating the reader, and evoking a response.

The remaining components of your package include the outside (or carrier) envelope, the reply envelope and the response device.

• Carrier Envelope

Size

Many nonprofits organizations, particularly smaller ones, use #10 carrier envelopes because these are the most familiar and accessible. But don't rule out smaller envelopes - the #9 and the monarch -- because the level of personal warmth seems to increase as the size of the envelope decreases.

Closed face or window

A closed face envelope is generally desirable since it looks more personal (assuming it is directly addressed and a label isn't applied to it). On the other hand, a window envelope (which tends to look businesslike) is preferable when you're using labels.

Teaser copy

Teaser copy is a headline or message appearing on the carrier envelope (Urgent Message Inside, for example). In general, don't use teaser copy if you're mailing first class; don't tease about something you can't deliver; and don't use banalities such as Open Today. In other words, if you don't have a really good teaser line or art, do without it.

• Reply envelope

As a general rule, it's smart to include an envelope for the prospective donor to use when returning a gift. He or she may not take the time otherwise. Some agencies provide a postage paid envelope (business reply envelope-BRE) while others do just as well with the donor applying postage.

• Response device

The response device is a slip or card which carries vital information. Its primary purpose is to enable you to identify the donor when he or she sends a gift.

The most effective response device contains: the name and address of the donor; the name and address of your organization; a statement about tax deductibility; a re-statement of your appeal (including a phrase such as "Yes, I want to do my share to help and enclosed is my gift of $___)"; and a listing of suggested gift amounts.

Tempted to enclose your agency's general brochure just for a little extra oomph? In most cases, don't. It'll save you money and, in a number of tests, a longer letter with no brochure outpulls the alternative. Why? Because if your letter is successful, if it builds to a climax and propels the reader to write you out a check, you don't want a three-panel review of your agency to block the momentum.

On the other hand, if the brochure genuinely comple- ments the theme of your letter -- say it's a case history vividly illustrating your agency's impact -- then that's a different matter.

PLEASE MR. POSTMAN

If you're a 501(c)(3) or a 501(c)(4) organization, obtain- ing a bulk rate mailing permit is routine. Simply submit the appropriate forms to your local postmaster. You will then have three choices when it comes to posting your agency's mail.

1) Pre-printing an indicia on your carrier envelope.

2) Metering each piece of mail.

3) Affixing a "live" precancelled stamp.

A plethora of tests have been conducted to determine whether a stamp outpulls the meter or the meter outpulls the indicia. As a general rule, both meter and stamp outpull the indicia and in some cases -- but not always -- the stamp outperforms the meter.

YOU CAN'T LICK ALL THE ENVELOPES

Now that you've decided to mail, you've selected your prospects and you've composed a masterful letter, the ques- tion is, "Who's going to do the detail work?" Who's going to print the letters; fold them; stuff, seal and post the envelopes; apply the labels, zip sort your mailing; and deliver the entire bundle to the post office?

If your mailing is small, say 3,000 pieces and fewer, you can manage it in-house (with the aid of some volunteers). For a larger mailing, you'll need a lettershop -- otherwise known as a mailing house. A full-service mailing house can both handle the "grunt work" of getting your mailing out and right from the start assist you with copywriting, materials, design, printing and list rentals.

WHEN TO MAIL?
In general, the best months for mailing are January, February, March, April, September, October and November.

If you're attempting to acquire new donors, avoid the three weeks before Christmas when donors receive numerous appeals from organizations they already support.

WHAT RESPONSE TO EXPECT?
If you're mailing to carefully selected prospects -- not your current donors -- you can expect anywhere from half a percent to two percent to contribute to your organization. *Be prepared to lose money or only recoup your costs.* This is often the nature of donor acquisition mailings.

However, of those who do contribute -- and here's where you begin to realize a profit -- about 50 percent will send you a second gift, and usually more than 60 percent of those giving a second gift will respond to a third appeal.

Some organizations, when mailing to their *donors*, succeed in renewing 80 percent of them annually. And many of these donors will, if treated properly, remain loyal for many years.

As for tracking the response to your mailing, you'll receive more than three-quarters of your total gifts by the end of the third week following your first return. You'll probably have all but a handful of the responses by the end of the sixth week.

WHOSE COMPUTER?
As it turns out, the response to your mailing is favorable. You're elated and relieved. "Is that all there is?" in the words of Peggy Lee. Not yet. You still must decide who's going to

maintain -- keep current, that is -- your donor list.

If you have the computer capabilities and the staff, you can maintain your file in-house (with help initially from a specialist).

If you don't have the in-house capability, you can hire a service bureau to perform a variety of computer services for you. Besides keeping your file updated, a service bureau can "source code" your donors (that is, code a gift as a memorial gift, a planned gift, a gift from a phonothon etc), furnish you with analyses of your contributors, produce labels, and much more.

HOW OFTEN CAN YOU ASK?

Tests have shown that when an organization waits too long to appeal for another gift, income from the renewal mailing actually *diminishes*. Whereas, new donors who receive a renewal request three to four months after their first gift tend to respond more generously. Generally speaking, you can expect donors to renew at a rate of between eight and 20 percent each time you appeal to them.

Don't be gun-shy about mailing frequently. If you genuinely need funds and can create strong appeals, you can succeed regardless of the number of requests you make.

SAYING THANKS

When a person makes a gift to you, he deserves to feel good about it and to be thanked. It's that simple really. Moreover, an effective thank-you letter is the key to holding onto a donor year after year, to raising his or her average gift amount, and to availing your organization of "bounce back" gifts (as many as 20 percent of your donors will send an additional gift if you enclose a reply envelope with your thank-you letter).

Don't procrastinate. You'll regret it.

HOW ARE YOU DOING?

To assess whether your appeal is effective, you must track how many people respond, how much money it brings in and what the average gift is.

After 60 days, tabulate your appeal using these categories:

❑ Number of pieces mailed.

❑ Number of gifts returned.

❑ Percent of response (divide the number of gifts returned by the number of pieces mailed).

❑ Gross income.

❑ Average gift (exclude major donors or your average will be skewed).

❑ Cost of mailing.

❑ Ratio of income to expense (divide your gross income by the cost of the mailing).

If you have mailed fewer than 3,000 pieces, your evaluation won't be statistically valid, but your instincts and the information you collect will enable you to make some educated guesses on your future mailing efforts.

WHAT SURVEYS SHOW

Surveys show fund raising mail is opened by approximately 72 percent of the people receiving it; women between the ages of 50 and 64 years are most apt to open it; women sign 75 to 95 percent of the checks.

10

Direct Mail: The World of Lists

Pick up the latest copy of SRDS Direct Marketing List Source (the mailing list catalog used most widely in the direct marketing field), and you'll find a compendium -- the girth of a phone book -- of thousands of lists you can rent.

Every list imaginable is there, from the conventional (American Express, MasterCard) to the obscure (San Francisco Music Box buyers, lovers of Mauna Loa nuts). From the tony (Sharper Image) to the tough (Harley-Davidson owners).

And just how many names would you like, ma'am? You can pinpoint several hundred or canvass the entire country. It's true, if you have the money and the desire, you can reach nearly every man, woman and child in the United States.

With the entire world - or rather, with all of America - at your fingertips, the issue isn't list availability - it's *list selection*. Just how among this plethora do you successfully identify the comparative handful of lists that'll work for you?

THE TYPES OF LISTS

Certainly a first step is understanding the three broad categories of lists that are available. These are 1) donor lists, 2) commercial lists, and 3) compiled lists.

Beginning with *donor lists*, this category is self evident. Often the most responsive, donor lists are comprised of people who, with their checkbook, have demonstrated their interest in a cause. They are comfortable sending money through the mail to support what they believe in (and as you'll see in a moment, that's an important hurdle).

Of course, simply because a person gives $50 to an animal rights group, that's no indication they'll give a similar amount, or anything at all, to a symphony appeal. So donor lists are most effective when the organization from whom they're rented is similar to your own, or when the profile of the contributors seems compatible with your own supporters.

Commercial lists are the second major type of list. Commercial lists are enormously varied and largely made up of magazine subscribers, book buyers, ticket purchasers, individuals who have bought merchandise through the mail, and the like. *Newsweek*, for example, will gladly rent you their list of subscribers; the Metropolitan Museum of Opera will share its ticket purchasers with you.

Commercial lists are valuable for the glimpse they give you into people's tastes, hobbies and interests. Whether that snapshot is a reliable predictor of their interest in your cause is another matter. Suffice it to say that commercial lists must be chosen with great care.

The final major type are *compiled lists*. Compiled lists are second generation lists, that is, they've been compiled from existing directories such as telephone books, voter rolls, motor vehicle registrations & county assessor records. The problems with compiled lists, as far as fund raising is concerned, are several.

First, they typically won't be as current as the original lists from which they're drawn; second, they can be so broad (i.e. individuals in Shelby County voting Republican in the last election) that without additional "overlays" such as income, age, and length of residency they're unpredictable; third, with singular exceptions, compiled lists aren't made up of people whose primary shared characteristic is spending money by mail.

From this cursory breakdown, it should be apparent that for most nonprofit organizations the types of lists that will usually pull best are donor lists, followed by carefully selected commercial lists, followed by compiled lists.

HOW DO YOU CHOOSE?

Becoming familiar with the kinds of lists available is a first step, but to truly feel at ease selecting the comparative handful of lists that are right for you requires much more.

First of all, it's necessary to understand that the lists you want to rent aren't usually available from the list owners directly. More often than not a list brokerage firm, of which there are hundreds throughout the country, will be in charge of managing them.

These firms, some of whom specialize in fund raising, serve as the intermediary between you and the list owner. They make the necessary arrangements (clearing mailing dates, negotiating volume discounts, handling paperwork) and for their efforts typically receive a 20 percent commission *from the owner* not from you. You normally pay the standard rental fee plus a nominal fee to the list broker for his or her assistance.

Incidentally, mailing lists are seldom for sale. They are rented to be used a single time for a pre-arranged cost per thousand names.

Any brokerage firm will be glad to send you a *data card* on the various lists they manage. And you should request one. A data card tells some basic and important facts. You'll learn, for example, the size of the list, the cost per thousand, the average gift or sale, and in what format the list can be supplied (i.e. labels, diskettes, magnetic tape).

Armed with these basics, you could roll the dice and place your order. But it might be a costly gamble, especially when you consider what you still *don't* know about the list, even with the data card in hand.

For example, you don't know the other organizations for whom the list works and doesn't work; you don't know what kinds of appeals or offers work best; you don't know the time of the year when the list pulls well; you don't know whether the list is truly up-to-date; you don't know if the list is overused; you don't know if the owner is reputable or reliable; in many cases you won't even know the actual name of the organization from whom the list comes (i.e. "dedicated humanitarians").

With a sizable sum of money at stake - anywhere from $50 to $200 per thousand names -- that's a lot to be in the dark about. Fortunately, a seasoned representative at the brokerage firm, or an independent list broker, will be able to answer these and other important questions for you. Failing to seek these experts' help can be risky, if not downright foolhardy.

But regardless of the approach you use -- seeking a list broker, using a full service mail house (that can also assist you in selecting lists), or going solo, you will want to carefully evaluate the following elements when examining any prospect list.

• *Mail responsiveness*

In general, your best prospects are those people who have already purchased, or contributed, by mail, whether a magazine subcription, an appeal for funds, or an item ordered via catalog.

Since surveys show that only about half of all Americans will send money by mail (except to pay taxes and other bills), mail responsiveness immediately reduces your universe of prospects and protects you from "mail junkies" (those who constantly send for catalogs and brochures with no intention to buy).

Before renting any list, be sure you know how many of the people have actually purchased or contributed, and whether the purchases or contributions were generated by direct mail or some other method (i.e. telephone solicitation, door-to-door canvass).

• *Currency*

One-fifth of Americans move every year. A full 20 percent. That startling statistic points out the overarching importance of keeping mailing lists current. If a list you're considering hasn't been updated within the past 12 months, be aware that its value to you will be significantly reduced. If the list hasn't been "cleaned" in the past three years, it may be practically useless.

A related problem to keep in mind is the accuracy of the list in terms of address changes and misspellings of names and addresses. If the list owner or service bureau maintaining the list is careless with its data entry program, not only will your mailing put off prospects (how personal is a letter when your name is misspelled?), but a high degree of nixies (undeliverable mail) and duplicates will affect your returns.

These two factors are important, but no more so than the following three:

• *Recency*

Recency refers to the year, month, or week when the individual on the list made his purchase or contribution.

Make sure the majority of the names are recent buyers or contributors.

• *Frequency*

Frequency indicates how often the individual has made a purchase or contribution in a particular time period. Choose those who have responded frequently.

• *Dollars*

Dollars of course refer to the total dollars spent or contributed, and the highest amount. Be wary of very small outlays, say of three, four, or five dollars. These individuals, even if they contribute, may not be worth the renewal cost to you.

TESTING IS THE KEY

How can you know for sure whether the mailing lists you've identified are the right ones for you?

Only one way can give you most of the answers: testing.

You may be convinced you know who your best prospects are, or you may be lulled into believing your list broker is infallible in this regard, but either or both of you could be totally wrong. Logic has been stood on its head quite often - - especially in the field of direct mail.

The prudent course is to test a sample of the lists you've pinpointed, and follow-up that test with a larger "roll-out" mailing of the lists that perform well.

For example, if your budget allows you to mail 25,000 pieces, you wouldn't risk all your money on one list. If it failed, not only would you have learned little, you wouldn't have uncovered any new possible sources of support. Instead, since a mailing of 5,000 generally gives a statistically valid reading of a list's responsiveness, you would likely use five lists of 5,000 names each. Then, if one or two of these pulled well, you'd have a larger universe to mail to, and odds are you'd pick up valuable clues to help you select other lists.

One caveat is in order here. Even when the response to a particular list exceeds your expectations, it's still wise to proceed with caution.You'll unquestionably want to rent additional names from that high-performing list, but you'll want to keep sampling other lists as well. Why? To keep mining new veins of support of course, but also because your roll-out of the list may be disappointing.

You may find your returns dropping for any number of reasons: bad timing, competing offers arriving in the mail with yours, or perhaps the brokerage firm didn't record the names you used in the test and included them again in your roll-out order. It's always best to keep your fingers in a number of pies.

HOW CRITICAL IS THE LIST?

There are a number of important components that will determine whether you succeed or fail in your direct mail appeals.

The lists you select, the power of your copy, the look of your package, the economic climate, even unpredictable circumstances like breaking news stories can affect your campaign in a positive or negative way.

Direct mail campaigns that succeed are able to integrate all of these elements, offering the right message to the right prospect at the right time requesting the right amount.

Still, if each of these elements were ranked in order of importance, none would be as crucial as the list you mail to. Superb copy and graphics can't save an appeal sent to the wrong list; while a mediocre package will often perform tolerably well when sent to authentic prospects.

11

Raising Money
by Telephone

On any given night, especially if your zip
code has been tagged a wealthy one, you probably receive
one or two calls either from businesses selling products or
organizations seeking your support.

Annoying or not, telemarketing works, which is why so
many organizations use this technique.

Is this method of fund raising for you? Who are the best
prospects to call? How much should you ask for?

These and a myraid of other questions, vital to
telemarketing success, are answered below.

MAJOR ADVANTAGES

There are a number of attractive benefits to calling
people. One, telephoning is more personal than direct mail;
your prospect has the feel of "personal contact." Two, you get
instant feedback on how the prospect is reacting to your
appeal, and can fine tune your approach as necessary. Three,
results are fast.The money usually arrives within a few days.
Four, a telemarketing campaign can involve scores of volun-

teers, who themselves are gift prospects for you. Five, unlike direct mail you know whether your appeal has reached your prospect. And, six, you can make your appeal locally, regionally, or nationally.

SOME DISADVANTAGES

For one thing, your prospect must have a listed number; many won't. Then too, the telephone isn't personal enough to solicit major gift prospects - the top 20 percent of the your donor pool. And, needless to say, the phone isn't very good for soliciting some types of gifts such as complex planned gifts.

THE BEST PROSPECTS

Generally speaking, telephoning for funds is best suited for existing or lapsed donors and members. They're already part of your family. Granted, you can acquire donors via the phone, but it won't be as cost-effective and the cost per contact will be greater than renewing or upgrading past donors or members.

Just how effective is the phone for renewing lapsed donors? Well, it's likely you can reinstate somewhere between 10 and 15 percent -- and at less cost than you'd normally spend to acquire a new donor through mail. Moreover, these reinstated donors can be put back into your mail program and their performance in future years will often mirror those who never strayed in the first place.

FINDING OTHER PROSPECTS

In addition to your constituents, there may be a number of people who are sympathetic to your cause. You find these prospects in the same way you find new prospects for a mailing: you rent and exchange lists (see Chapter 10). These might include lists of donors to similar causes, lists of people who subscribe to various publications, lists compiled according to certain demographics, lists of special interest groups, lists of people who have purchased particular products and services. Most likely you'll need a list broker to help you choose from among the thousands of lists available.

SHOULD YOU CALL TOP PROSPECTS?

Your top prospects -- those on whom you depend for major gifts -- shouldn't be solicited by phone. Nor by mail for that matter. Unless it's absolutely impossible, they should be accorded the respect of a personal visit.

GETTING PHONE NUMBERS

The fastest way to get phone numbers you don't have is to hire a commercial firm. Typically you submit your list to them -- on floppy disks or computer tape -- and they match it against their own files (containing tens of millions of names). A good percentage of the phone numbers you need can be found this way.

VOLUNTEERS OR PAID CALLERS?

To determine this, you must weigh various advantages and disadvantages. First the advantages. Using volunteers saves money; volunteer callers are usually enthusiastic about your cause and eager to become good callers; and some prospects are more generous when called by volunteers.

Now the disadvantages. Your turnover rate will be high; other responsibilities -- home, school, and career -- will cause some volunteers to beg off at the last minute; some won't work diligently or they'll be sensitive to criticism; and you won't usually have an easy time finding enough volunteers.

If you're only planning a few telemarketing sessions, you're probably better off using volunteers. But if yours is an extended program, it might be easier and more profitable to consider paid callers.

HOW MANY CALLERS?

Twenty-five numbers per hour - that's what a good caller should be able to dial (not reach, but dial). So divide the number of names on your prospect list by 25, and you'll have the number of callers you'll need. Of course, as many as half of the numbers won't answer and another percentage will be wrong numbers. So keep in mind that your good callers may only be able to reach and talk with maybe 10 prospects an hour.

HOW LONG CALLING?

Assuming you're working with volunteer callers, three-hour stretches are about the maximum.

CALLER TRAINING

Don't kiss cash good-bye by turning a caller loose with little or no instruction. Instead, plan a training session that focuses on the general nature of fund raising, why people give, the case for supporting your cause, your current dollar goals, and how funds you raise will be used.

Needless to say, you'll want to devote time to calling techniques, how to handle the paperwork, details of the incentives you're offering, information about publicity, and what your callers can generally expect.

OFFERING INCENTIVES TO CALLERS

Whether they're volunteers or paid, you want to reward the performance of exceptional callers. For short-term performance, consider small prizes you can award the same day such as tee shirts or a bottle of wine. For motivating long-term performance, a more substantial gift such as a watch or dinner for two is fitting.

Prizes might be given for any number of accomplishments including:

- First pledge of the session
- First pledge over $100
- Highest number of pledges
- Largest pledge obtained
- Highest pledge dollar total
- Highest average number of calls per session
- Highest percentage of positive responses
- Highest average gift

THE BEST SET-UP FOR CALLERS

There's a range of opinion on this. Those who supervise extended phonothons, involving a limited number of paid callers, often suggest cubicle arrangements. On the other hand, people who organize large, one-night or one-week efforts, especially those using volunteer callers, tend to favor a big, somewhat noisy, open room (allowing excitement to build).

Regardless of your preference, there's universal agreement that placing callers in separate rooms is a bad idea. The group spirit is lost, supervision becomes a problem, and the caller's enthusiasm tends to wane noticeably.

THE ATMOSPHERE TO STRIVE FOR

Phonothons need an atmosphere of fun, excitement, and bustle. Then, success is infectious and gifts seem to flow in. A simple tactic such as giving your callers bells to ring whenever a prospect promises a gift will boost spirits and profits too.

SHOULD CALLERS HAVE A SCRIPT?

There are some convincing reasons for using a script: It

prompts you, the organizer, to think through your appeal; it's a confidence booster for callers, showing them how you want to present your cause; it ensures a degree of uniformity; callers usually complete their calls faster; and a script tends to keep the conversation on track. Nevertheless, to maintain believability, callers might more effectively use the script as an outline rather than words to be read verbatim.

VOLUNTEER ANXIETY

Since an early refusal will chill a caller's performance -- sometimes for the whole evening -- successful phonothon leaders stack the deck. They make sure, when handing out prospect cards, that some easy prospects are right on top. That way, your caller's chances for a quick "yes" -- and a fruitful evening -- are vastly improved.

ASKING FOR A SPECIFIC AMOUNT

Specificity is the key in telephone fund raising. Insist that your callers avoid open-ended questions such as "Can you pledge?" or "Do you want to pledge?" or "What can you give?" or "Can you give less?" If the prospect hesitates or refuses to give at the level requested, ask for a smaller, specific gift. To do otherwise is to relinquish control of the conversation.

WHAT AMOUNT SHOULD YOU REQUEST?

One way is to use the rule of five, that is, if you expect a $25 pledge, start out with a $125 request. Or, said differently, to win big pledges, you have to ask for big pledges. This approach, scary to some volunteers, will alert your prospects that you're seeking something substantial, and it'll give your callers a great deal of negotiating room (the key to attracting big pledges). If the prospect commits at the top level, well and good. If the response is negative, move quickly to the next level.

WHEN THE PROSPECT ISN'T AVAILABLE

Even though it's tempting to talk to whomever answers the phone, resist the temptation. Save your efforts for the prospect. Not only is he or she the one who's received your publicity, but another member of the household will rarely negotiate seriously. When the talk turns to money, he or she will pass the buck.

TAKING PLEDGES VIA CREDIT CARD

Pledges by credit card are ideal, if your organization is equipped to handle them. Once you've recorded the prospect's card number and validated it, the pledge is no longer a pledge, it's money in the bank. Moreover, your prospect isn't likely to back out of a credit card pledge even if a financial hardship arises.

SHOULD I USE PUBLICITY?

The best phonothons don't make cold calls; instead, publicity of some sort always precedes the period of calling. Maybe it's a simple postcard or one-page note. Then, too, some organizations send sophisticated multi-page letters. The idea, of course, is to match the publicity to the income potential.

For a small phonothon seeking annual support, a notice in your newsletter might suffice. Whereas, a multi-million dollar drive could very well warrant personal letters and every other means of publicity at your disposal.

THE BEST TIME TO CALL

If you're calling the prospect at work, the hours between 9 a.m. and noon, and 2 and 5 p.m., are usually the best. For prospects you hope to reach at home, most organizers schedule their calling between 6 and 9 p.m. If possible, consider calling your prospects over the weekend, for you can sometimes double or triple the coverage. The best times then are between 11 a.m. and 5:30 p.m. and 7 p.m. to 9 p.m.

HOW MUCH WILL IT COST?

Some telemarketing campaigns, costing as much as 70 cents per dollar raised, have been considered successful. Even those costing more, upwards of 90 cents, have pleased their organizations.

But most organizers agree that an efficient telemarketing campaign shouldn't cost more than 30 to 40 cents per dollar raised. Keep this benchmark figure in mind as you plan your budget.

WILL YOU SUCCEED?

When all is said and done, the single most important factor in telemarketing is your cause. Granted, your organizational and management skills count, but your ultimate success or failure really depends on the credibility, mission, and reputation of your organization. All else is secondary.

12

The Capital Campaign

Consider how capital fund raising has evolved. Not many years ago, goals of $5 million and $10 million were thought to be ambitious. Today, they soar as high as $1 *billion*.

Organizations which used to conduct a campaign every 10 or 20 years now gear up for yet another push within six or seven.

And not solely for "bricks and mortar" as in the past. Today, items such as salaries, expanded endowment, and even operating expenses are folded into the campaign.

Too, the length of campaigns has increased. Whereas, three to five years was the norm, today a 10-year campaign isn't uncommon.

And, finally, the focus of solicitations has shifted. No longer is *everyone* a prospect, as in "community chest" days. Now only the wealthiest 10 to 20 percent get sustained attention.

But, the more things change, as the French say, the more they stay the same. And what has remained the same, despite any changes, is this: you cannot enter into a capital campaign without extensive thought and planning -- much of it completed before any campaign is announced.

Are you ready to tackle fund raising's most formidable challenge? After reading what follows, you should have a better sense.

DETERMINING YOUR READINESS

As a general rule, until your development program is established, you shouldn't think in terms of a capital campaign. It's far better to build your reputation and your volunteer leadership so that your first campaign effort has a realistic chance of success.

But even if yours is an established organization, you still need to ask yourself three pertinent questions:

1) Is there a genuine need to conduct the campaign (is there some urgency to it, in other words)?

2) Do you have enough prospects with enough potential to call upon? And,

3) Are there sufficient volunteers on your board to lead the drive?

If your answer to any of these questions is "no," then it's doubtful you will succeed.

ANCILLARY BENEFITS

A successful capital campaign will, of course, raise money but it will have additional benefits as well, such as:

❑ *Increased board commitment*

Almost always, the quality and commitment of your board leadership will be improved ... and empowered to some degree.

❑ *New board candidates*

Some community leaders, uninvolved with you before, will now be willing to join your board or become actively involved.

❑ *Enhanced staff skills*
Your staff, as a result of a disciplined campaign, will be more effective with respect to the annual fund.

❑ *Giving levels increase*
Your current donors will have their giving sights raised and, by giving more, will become even stronger supporters of your organization.

❑ *Donor base expanded*
Some new donors who contribute to your capital campaign will show interest in what you do and can be included in future annual fund solicitations.

HOW TO PREPARE

Whether your campaign succeeds or fails depends largely on what you do ahead of time.

And, what you must do before launching any campaign is:

1) Identify your community leaders, the "movers and shakers" who make things happen.

2) Find from among this group desirable leadership, that is, those with the right status and connections.

3) Identify potential workers and committee members.

4) Glean as much as you can about the levels of support you can expect to receive and where any big money will come from.

Considering the importance of pre-campaign activities, it's not unusual to begin planning two or three years before the formal kickoff of a campaign. It's common, too, to have pledges and commitments of a third or more of the goal before any public announcement.

ANNUAL FUND, CAPITAL CAMPAIGN, OR BOTH?

Even in the midst of a capital campaign, an organization must still pursue annual operating funds.

Most donors today know that, but it can still be a challenge to conduct a capital and an annual campaign in the same year. Fortunately, there are three principal solutions to this dilemma.

1) As part of your capital campaign goal, include the money you would ordinarily raise for annual operating expenses. This allows for a single solicitation.

2) Use the double ask, by having your volunteers request both a capital *and* an annual gift. The upside is the personalized treatment your donors are accorded; the downside is that some solicitors will be uncomfortable with this approach.

3) Use the separate ask, by having a different corps of volunteers -- who won't be easy to find, of course -- make your pitch for an annual fund gift.

Whatever option you choose, it's not unusual for a capital campaign to raise your donors' giving sights and lead to larger annual fund contributions as well.

TIMING

Despite a poor or robust economy, the best time to start a capital campaign is when you've done everything necessary to prepare yourself.

There's little evidence to suggest that economic conditions affect voluntary support. In fact, there's evidence to the contrary, that despite the climate on Wall Street -- or Main Street -- Americans respond when there's an authentic need. Notwithstanding the naysayers, no time is ever a bad time to start raising money.

LEADERSHIP: THE VITAL INGREDIENT

Selecting the best volunteer leadership is probably the most important component for ensuring the success of any capital campaign.

For every individual you're considering, ask yourself the

following questions:
1) Is this individual respected by colleagues?
2) Does he or she have the stature to attract others?
3) Will this person give, and at what level?
4) Will he or she solicit others?
5) Will the person devote the required amount of time?

If you're fortunate enough to recruit high-calibre leadership, involve them only in important decisions, such as approving your case, goal-setting, recruiting of other leadership, and the selection of professional counsel. Asking them to do nitty-gritty details is a waste of their time and talent.

WILL YOU NEED PROFESSIONAL COUNSEL?

Few organizations have the professional staff needed to conduct -- or to give undivided attention to -- a capital campaign. Whereas a fund raising counselor, experienced in capital campaigns, can step in and develop a plan, conduct a feasibility study, help fashion the strongest case, suggest the goal, outline the leadership and volunteer needs, and establish a timetable and a realistic budget.

And if all that weren't important enough, counsel also serves in another capacity, that of catalyst, seeing to it that the right things happen at the right time to assure your success.

Understand, the time to employ counsel is *at the very beginning*. Better than any staff person, this outsider can stand before your board and say, "Unless you're committed to this campaign and give sacrificially of your money *and* your time, there will be little or no chance for success."

HOW MUCH IT WILL COST

How much will a capital campaign cost? Some major organizations with seasoned staff and good track records of fund raising can raise capital funds for as little as three percent of the goal.

Other organizations, particularly smaller ones unable to attract lead gifts of six- and seven-figures, may spend anywhere from five to 10 percent.

Many factors will influence what you spend, and among the most important are:

❑ The amount of money you're attempting to raise.
❑ How many prospects you have.
❑ What your plans are for cultivating your prospects.
❑ Professional counsel.
❑ Where your prospects live (close by or far away?).
❑ The length of your drive.
❑ Your current level of support.

In terms of needing dollars up front, a capital campaign is expensive. However, in terms of cost per dollar raised, it can be an extremely efficient approach.

ARE YOUR PLANS FEASIBLE?

A feasibility study is a survey of key members of your constituency to determine whether your organization is ready for a major funds drive.

Properly conducted feasibility studies will provide answers to a number of key questions, such as:

❑ Does your cause have validity and appeal?
❑ Do you have qualified volunteer and staff leadership?
❑ How much money can you expect to raise?
❑ How long will it take? And,
❑ How much will your campaign cost?

Since the campaign will provide answers to these questions, why, you might ask, spend money doing a survey? Because you don't want to fail due to poor planning, or a limited prospect pool, or lack of leadership, or insufficient funds to launch a drive, or because you announced a goal so high it scared away all your potential supporters.

A good feasibility study also looks internally and seeks to

answer questions about your organization. Is your board effective? Have you been gaining or losing donors? Do you have leadership capable of raising big money? How experienced is your development staff? What records do you have? And, do you have a viable program of cultivating donors and recognizing their generosity?

The question is often asked, Can an organization conduct its own feasibility study or is a consultant needed?

The consultant certainly has one big advantage: he or she can ask hard questions and get hard answers.

Prospects are more likely to share with an outsider any doubts they have about your organization or any lack of confidence in your leaders. Also, they are usually more comfortable discussing their financial intentions.

SETTING YOUR GOAL

In setting a campaign goal you must strike a balance between the needs of your organization and the perceived wherewithal of your constituents.

As such, a realistic goal is based upon three factors:

1) Your need for funds, convincingly presented.

2) The perception of your organization and people's appreciation for what you've accomplished.

3) Your campaign organization, that is, your plans, leadership, professional help, and the like.

Unless, as part of your pre-campaign preparation, you can outline a "table of gifts" showing the size and number of contributions you'll need to succeed, and unless your feasibility study has identified legitimate prospects for each, it is difficult, if not impossible, to set a goal you can reasonably expect to attain.

What you don't want to do is to add up your needs and simplistically accept that that amount is possible to raise. That may be a first step, but unless you verify your goal by careful and pragmatic research, it is naive to proceed based on needs and hopes alone.

FROM THE TOP DOWN, AND INSIDE OUT

To be effective, fund raising must be "top down and inside out."

"Top down" means you solicit the largest gift first, since it will set a pattern for the remaining gifts. If the top gift is too low, other gifts will drop accordingly and your campaign will be compromised.

"Inside out" means that your organization's inner family is solicited first. Only when this phase is completed, does the campaign reach out to other constituencies.

Sequential solicitation, as this strategy is known, is a necessity in capital campaigns. It requires restraint, to be sure, but it forces you to focus on larger gifts and discourages undue attention on smaller ones.

THE 90/10 RULE

For decades, planners of capital campaigns have been guided by the principle that the first 10 gifts in a campaign should equal one third of the goal, the next 100 gifts should equal one third, and all of the remaining gifts should account for the final third.

But this "rule of thirds" has been modified, except for very small campaigns. Today's capital drives expect to secure 90 percent or more from 10 percent of the donors. This often means that at least one gift of 10 percent of the goal, and two gifts each of five percent, must be sought at the very beginning of the campaign.

WINDFALL GIFTS: DON'T BE DELUDED

While a carefully planned and orchestrated campaign will often produce a few windfall gifts, only the foolhardy anticipate these pleasant surprises.

Should mega gifts come your way, rejoice. But if they don't, your well-conceived campaign will raise money anyway.

BOARD COMMITMENT

Financial investment and participation - without these twin commitments from each member of your governing board, it will be difficult, if not impossible, to motivate others to back your cause wholeheartedly.

In fact, unanimous participation and sacrificial giving are so essential that you'd be wise to delay your campaign until all board members understand that, until they make a full commitment to the effort, few others will be inspired to do so.

INVOLVE YOUR TOP PROSPECTS

One of the best ways to ensure the success of your campaign is to get your best prospects involved from the outset. Involvement almost invariably leads to commitment and financial support.

A fundamental tenet, when organizing a capital campaign, is to put your best prospects -- usually those closest to your organization -- on the major volunteer committees.

See to it that these key prospects attend strategy sessions that inform and commit them to the success of your campaign.

WHAT YOU DON'T KNOW WILL HURT YOU

An integral part of the planning for any capital campaign -- in which all participants should be involved -- is prospect identification and evaluation.

Such research may take weeks or even months. Its purpose is threefold: to determine how much the prospect could give if he or she were sufficiently interested, to discover what would motivate the person to give generously, and to learn who could most effectively solicit the gift.

The preparation for each major gift prospect should be organized as a campaign in itself, especially since 75 to 80 percent of the goal of many capital drives comes from a very small pool of donors.

Solicitation itself is withheld until the best possible volunteer is equipped with the most persuasive arguments that research has uncovered.

THE PRINTED WORD

Perhaps the single most important document of a capital campaign is the case statement. It answers all the important questions about your campaign, presents your arguments for support, explains the plan for raising money, shows how gifts may be made, and identifies the people who are leading the drive. In sum, it tells all that needs to be told (See Chapter 3).

As for other publications, they should be tasteful but understand that even masterful efforts get little more than fleeting attention.

What can be useful are progress reports, issued weekly or bi-weekly. These let your workers know what's been accomplished and what's left to do. Moreover, since no one wants to look bad among peers, they can serve to stimulate action.

PUTTING IT ALL TOGETHER

In sum, to be successful in capital fund raising, you must have:

❏ Support, in the form of money and time, from all key groups.

❏ An organization with a clear image and a plan for growth.

❏ Realistic objectives based on legitimate needs.
❏ A persuasive case for support.
❏ A feasibility study examining your preparedness, both internally and externally.
❏ Top level, trained volunteers.
❏ Major donors ready to give substantial lead gifts.

To the extent that any of these vital factors is missing, your ability to conduct a successful capital campaign will be seriously impaired.

13

Donor Gift Clubs

Psychology has always played an incalculable role in fund raising.

Volumes have been written, for instance, on the motivations for giving, dissecting every philanthropic impulse from the love of God to the fear of tyrannical bosses.

But perhaps no aspect of fund raising exploits psychology so well as donor clubs. Originating in colleges and universities, such clubs have since spread to hospitals, museums, and even voluntary health agencies.

It's easy to understand why these clubs are so successful. They fulfill a host of human desires and needs, not the least of which are our need to feel connected and our desire to be treated special.

What follows is a thorough look at this profitable vehicle, one that should help you enhance your existing club or light the way for starting a new one.

MOTIVATION AND GIFT CLUBS

Motivating prospects to give, and to give at greater and greater levels, is a necessary factor in fund raising. This need to motivate is, in fact, what led to the creation of gift clubs.

Gift clubs not only set the giving bar, as it were, they motivate donors to increase their current levels of giving or to make substantial first-time gifts.

You will generally find that three basic needs arouse most of your gift club members.

• *The need to feel important.*

Being a member of the President's Council or the Blue Ribbon 100 is not only satisfying to the ego, it makes your members feel important when supporting your cause.

• *The need for appreciation.*

We all like to be appreciated, especially for doing something so hard as parting with our money. Well-run gift clubs, those liberal with special treatment or tasteful (inexpensive) gifts, satisfy this desire for recognition.

• *The need to be liked.*

By touting their accomplishments in your newsletter, by sending them invitations to special programs, by remembering their birthdays and anniversaries, you will let your members know you care about them and they will reward you amply for it.

Satisfy these three elemental needs and your gift club members will be loyal for life.

PURPOSES

The principal goal of a gift club is to increase your level of unrestricted income (many organizations *only* allow unrestricted gifts to their gift clubs).

But this isn't the only advantage, for a successful gift club also:

❑ Provides a ready-made reason to ask donors to upgrade their gifts.

❑ Lends added prestige to your appeal.

❑ Offers you a way to specially recognize your major donors.

❑ Deepens the commitment of your major donors because of the special treatment they're accorded.

❑ Attracts new donors who are influenced by the recognition given club members.

❑ Enables you to hold social events for club members, thereby further cultivating their interest in your cause.

❑ Creates an ideal market for planned gifts since your best planned giving prospects are those having a continuing relationship with you.

❑ Identifies and develops volunteers to serve as fund raising leaders.

When all is said and done, a gift club is but one more way for you to focus on your top donors, that 10 to 20 percent who inevitably contribute most of your gift income.

CLUB ORGANIZATION

In most cases, you'll find it helpful to organize your gift club under the leadership of a steering committee.

This committee will be charged with:

1) Promoting the objectives of your club.

2) Increasing membership each year by identifying and soliciting individuals who qualify. And,

3) Developing and overseeing a program that nurtures a rewarding relationship between members and your organization.

According to your needs and the size of your club, you might have a new donor committee that welcomes new members, a prospect committee that makes recommendations for new people, an activities committee to plan events and, finally, an annual dinner committee to orchestrate your yearly event.

SETTING THE GIVING LEVELS

When establishing your gift categories, look carefully for

trends in giving to your organization. If you set levels too high, you'll scare rather than challenge your prospects. The following suggestions should help:

1) Count your total number of prospects and donors.

2) Count your number of donors.

3) Calculate how many of your current donors give at the levels of $10-99, $100-249, $250-499, $500-999, $1,000 and up.

4) Based on this calculation, you should be able to estimate at what levels you can expect the greatest number of donors to increase their gifts, with the fewest number decreasing theirs.

Say for example, someone regularly gives $200 annually. If you were to set two levels, one at $100 and another at $500, what might she do - increase her gift to $500 or decrease it to $100? Depending on your particular circumstances, and your sense of what each donor might do, you may very well consider a $250 level.

5) Your final step is to review all of your (non-donor) prospects -- using a group of people who know something about them -- and rate each, whether at $50 or $1,000.

This process should allow you to set your giving levels, albeit imperfectly.

One final note: by including bequests and other forms of planned giving among the ways your prospect can meet the gift requirement, you'll motivate many to think about their estates in relation to you.

SPECIAL BENEFITS

People tend to give to organizations that offer them real or imagined benefits pertaining to their personal needs.

The range of benefits you offer is of course limited only by your budget, but some of the more popular include:

- *Newsletters, magazines, or journals*

Typically gift club members receive a free subscription to one or more of your house publications.

• *Access to special programs, events, or services*

You might make certain programs or services available only to members (for example, a symphony may have a Members Only room).

• *Discounts on programs, services, and products*

Your members might receive discounts on courses, cruises, and any products you sell.

Keep in mind, when you're considering new or existing benefits, two considerations:

1) Your goal is to provide the most attractive benefits at the lowest possible cost, and

2) *Perceived value* greatly influences your members' evaluation of a benefit. A certificate or plaque, costing you little, can be extremely important to your donors - sometimes more so than any glossy magazine.

BASELINE BENEFITS

Regardless of your range of giving levels, some benefits should be available to everyone. For example:

❑ All donors should get receipts (for your records, and for theirs).

❑ Ask donors at the higher giving levels if they'd mind publicity. Many won't mind at all (in fact they'll be tickled to receive it).

❑ Have your donors okay all press releases about them.

❑ Keep your donors informed by sending cultivation materials about your organization's achievements and needs. Further, if there's an activity in which you believe they have an interest, be sure to invite them.

❑ Let your donors know you value them for more than their money by calling upon them, when possible, to serve as guest speakers, committee members, volunteers, and the like.

WHO QUALIFIES?

There's really only one qualification for membership in a gift club: that an individual give to your organization annually.

That said, you will still need some parameters. For example, when an individual's gift is matched by a company, does the additional amount entitle the donor for membership at a higher gift level, or do only personal gifts qualify? Is your club open to individuals alone or can corporations join? Must the gift be unrestricted? Do planned gifts figure in? How about gifts to an endowment campaign?

Establish whatever ground rules will attract the most gifts, but be clear and adhere to them.

Moreover, remember one elementary fact: you create gift clubs for the benefit of your organization. Stay flexible enough so that you can enlist the people you most need to enlist such as potential major donors who require further cultivation.

FINDING MEMBERS

Before starting a gift club, you'll need to develop a realistic list of prospects for each giving category. And, of course, the best place to start is in your own backyard, with your board members, staff, and current donors.

Once this list is in order, you can then proceed to your inner family's friends and associates, former supporters, and finally to businesses, and the community at large.

You will, generally speaking, need four or five *qualified* prospects for every one person you hope to enroll.

Two approaches you may find helpful are member-get-a-member campaigns, if you have a highly motivated core group, and a nominating campaign whereby current members are asked to nominate likely candidates.

ENLISTING MEMBERS

Once you've established your gift club goals, developed a

convincing case as to why prospects should join, and set your giving categories, you're ready enlist your prospects.

Begin with the following three steps:

1) Enlist people in your highest categories first. Otherwise a $100 contributor might have enrolled at $500 had she been approached with this higher category first.

2) Solicit your prospects face-to-face. Don't rely on a mailed invitation except in your lowest categories. Granted, some higher level prospects may respond to mail, but the surest approach is still the personal one.

3) Don't give up easily on less than receptive prospects. The right person asking at the right time for the right reason can achieve wonders.

One final note: it's important, when soliciting new members, to assign to volunteers those prospects who are expected to give at the same level the volunteer has given. This means, in essence, that no solicitor should make a call before making his own gift.

PRINTED MATERIALS

First and foremost you'll need a document that convincingly explains why someone should join your gift club. This "case," which speaks to the heart of your organization's mission, will be featured in one form or another in all of your materials and will help trustees, volunteers, and staff understand and promote your program.

Secondly, a special newsletter for club members can be fruitful, one that reports on club activities, new members, and significant programs and services offered by your organization.

Thirdly, to give your club added cache, you might publish a booklet outlining your goals and listing members from the previous year. The idea is to reinforce the feeling among members that they are a small, prestigious group especially important to you.

Finally, you might want a tasteful invitation to hand to each prospect personally, or to mail immediately following the call. Your invitation should concisely restate your case and outline the benefits of membership.

Keep in mind that whatever their form, successful gift club materials typically include: 1) the objective of your club, 2) the criteria for membership, 3) a compelling case, 4) a gift reply form and return envelope, 5) a listing of current members and steering committee, and 6) governing board members.

LEADERSHIP

A strong board chairperson can be instrumental to your gift club. He or she can best present the program to your trustees and enlist their participation, recruit a gift club chairperson, invite various individuals to join, invite members to special events and participate in them, and communicate regularly with members.

The staff, too, has important responsibilities. These include: outlining the program (its purpose, membership qualifications, and benefits); identifying prospects; preparing printed materials; coordinating solicitations; reporting progress; overseeing events; keeping on top of pledge reminders and gift acknowledgments; and, of course, maintaining accurate records.

◆◆◆

Starting a gift club is really quite simple. All you need are enough *genuine* prospects who have the wherewithal, if motivated, to give generously, a set of policies and procedures, and some tastefully printed materials.

Despite their simplicity, however, gift clubs are highly attractive vehicles, allowing you not only to increase your revenue but, as importantly, to:

1) Build loyalty by giving members a greater sense of

ownership in your organization;

2) Deepen commitment by making members feel they are important beyond the dollars they give;

3) Prepare people to continue their support, since renewal is anticipated each year; and,

4) Solicit a higher-quality donor, as club members will typically stay with you longer than other donors.

All said, gift clubs harbor great potential for nearly every type of organization.

14

Researching Foundations

Most development professionals would readily acknowledge the obvious benefits of knowing as much as possible about a potential grantor — or any prospective donor, for that matter. Yet a systematic, organized foundation research effort is undertaken by relatively few development offices — this despite the fact that at least 50 percent of successful foundation solicitation is research.

For many fund raisers, research consists of little more than a cursory glance through this or that directory searching for every foundation that funds a particular field of interest: "Aha, the Cure-All Foundation seeks to promote human welfare, let's send them a proposal."

But take a closer look at Cure-All and you might discover that despite its broad mission, the foundation is really only interested in funding literacy programs for Romanian refugees, or some other very specific niche.

Unless your organization just happens to provide that service, your proposal is a waste of everyone's time. And it has the potential to be more damaging than you might think.

WHY IS RESEARCH SO IMPORTANT?

It can be tempting to send proposals to every possible foundation prospect with even the slimmest connection to your organization's cause. After all, technology has made such a mass mailing approach easy; your computer churns out numerous copies of your standard proposal and you simply wait for the law of averages to land in your favor. Further, many foundations now accept proposals via the Internet. At least one of these is sure to give you a grant, right?

Not necessarily. With competition for grant dollars keener than ever, most foundations are inundated with proposals and thus able to pick and choose carefully the programs they wish to fund. A computer-generated proposal -- easily recognizable by any seasoned foundation officer -- stands little chance of review, much less funding.

Furthermore, such a boilerplate approach clearly speaks to the lack of effort your organization has made to match your programs with the foundation's purpose. Not only do you lose out on funding possibilities, your organization also risks developing a reputation for careless and slovenly management.

The best proposal carefully and determinedly explores why your organization's program or service is a perfect match for the foundation's current interests or priorities - current being the operative word.

While most directories do list the foundation's mission or purpose, these entries are often purposely broad to allow the foundation's trustees flexibility to change emphases as needs arise.

A foundation may list health programs among its priorities, for example, but decide to direct this year's funding solely to leukemia programs. Most directories don't allow for these timely distinctions, so more homework would be necessary to uncover such vital information - especially if your organization conducts leukemia research.

Clearly, methodical foundation research will greatly improve your chances of funding, but it's true that budget and staff limitations often inhibit such an effort. While large universities and hospitals can assign these arduous and painstaking tasks to their corporate and foundation relations departments, most organizations don't have that luxury.

Foundation research often falls to the same development staff who plan the annual campaign, coordinate special events, and oversee the organization's direct mail program.

But even small development shops can institute a more organized and uniform approach to foundation research using the steps outlined below. Any attempts to more clearly identify your top foundation prospect will increase your odds of securing a grant and therefore are well worth the effort.

BEFORE YOU BEGIN

Some say that effective foundation research requires an eagle eye, a detective's nose, and the patience of a saint. While these desired characteristics may be a bit overstated, it is true that a prospect researcher will benefit from these varied skills.

Your eagle eye, for example, can help you discern patterns and similarities among a foundation's grantees or unearth a familiar name on the trustee list.

A detective's nose is needed to snoop out information not always readily available or to cross check a number of sources searching for a common funding theme or emphasis.

But all of this time-consuming snooping is worthless without the patience to diligently record all of the pertinent facts you ultimately uncover.

WHERE TO START

The most obvious place to begin your research is also the most often overlooked: your own institution.

Since the goal of foundation research is to identify the foundations likeliest to fund your programs, it is vital that you have some basis for making that judgment. Before you begin to search for your organization's perfect funding match, arm yourself with detailed answers to the following:

1) What is your organization's mission or case statement? What are your goals, both broad and specific?

2) What is your organization's long-range plan? What does the agency hope to accomplish in the next five, 10, or 15 years?

3) What other sources of funding do you receive? This includes not only other foundations, corporations, and government support, but the level of financial commitment of your board, your members, or other constituents as well?

4) What programs or projects, both existing and planned, lend themselves to foundation funding?

5) How is your organization unique, innovative, or distinctive?

6) Are your programs cost-efficient? You should have accurate budget information for your organization for at least the past three years.

7) Do you comply with all regulations regarding your nonprofit status, affirmative action plans, and other state and federal legislation that might affect your organization?

Once you have a clear picture of the needs and capabilities of your organization, you are ready to search for the foundations that most closely align themselves with your cause.

RECORDKEEPING

The unavoidable -- yet essential -- bane of every development officer's professional life, paperwork is no less important to your foundation research effort. The best research effort will not compensate for, and indeed will be sabotaged by, a poorly managed recordkeeping system.

Each fact you uncover through your research should be viewed as a key that may open the foundation's coffers to your organization, and should be treated as a valuable commodity. Seemingly inconsequential information of little interest to you now may become critical in six months or a year as your organization's priorities change or expand.

It is well worth the effort to record as much data about the foundation as possible. Such diligence may not only help you later but will also ensure continuity for your organization in the face of staff turnover.

In addition, careful recordkeeping will allow you to share important information about prospective funders with your organization's executives, board members, and other volunteers, all valuable allies in the solicitation process.

Foundation records can be simple or complex, depending upon the staff time you have to spare for the effort. Some organizations not only maintain individual files on each of its 50 or 100 top foundation prospects, but also a separate system summarizing the pertinent data in each file.

For organizations seeking funding for several different projects, a grid which overlays all of your funding needs with foundation prospects that offer grants for those areas can organize your prospects concisely and clearly.

And still other organizations, those with an active foundation solicitation program, can benefit from a rolling calendar, which organizes information about proposal deadlines, formats, and foundation contacts.

THE EVALUATION FORM

But if limited staff and budgets don't allow for such sophisticated recordkeeping systems, it's best to concentrate your efforts on preparing one standardized form for recording information about your top foundation prospects.

This evaluation form, along with a foundation's annual report (if available), copies of correspondence with the foundation, and any other pertinent information will comprise your research record of each of your primary prospects. The form should allow for the following entries regarding each foundation:

- Name, address, and telephone number
- Contact person
- Trustees or staff
- History or background -- why was the foundation established? What is its stated mission or purpose?
- Type of foundation -- community, private or family, corporate, general purpose, and the like
- Specific areas of interest
- Geographic focus
- Type of support (capital, operating, seed money)
- Current assets
- Last year's grant expenditures and number of grants
- Sample grants and recent grants to organizations with programs similar to yours
- Prior contact with your organization (including past grants, rejected proposals, and any other correspondence)
- Board meeting dates and proposal deadlines
- Trustee connections to your organization

This is the basic data you need for each of your top foundation prospects.

RESOURCES

While there are numerous foundation resources and references available -- check your local library, especially if it is part of *The Foundation Center's Cooperating Collections Network* -- as a careful foundation researcher you will need to employ your best sleuthing skills to ferret out the most recent, accurate information possible. It's best, of course, not to rely solely on one source but rather to supplement and verify your data by consulting several different sources.

Your goal, throughout the research process, is to continuously distill the information you uncover until you have winnowed down your prospect list to only those foundations that meet your criteria. Does the foundation support your field of interest? Your geographical area? The type of support you seek? A "no" to any of these questions immediately eliminates the foundation from consideration.

By consulting any of a number of foundation directories published periodically -- many which list foundations alphabetically and have cross-referenced indexes of subjects of interest and geographical areas of interest -- you should be able to narrow your foundation prospect list to a manageable number.

The next crucial step in your information gathering process is to track down anything published by the foundation itself. These may include the following: annual report, brochure, application guidelines, newsletters, or news releases.

Here, you will find a more descriptive picture of what the foundation actually funds as opposed to its broad statement of purpose in a directory listing.

Most annual reports also include a list of grant recipients, helpful in detecting patterns of giving, a concentration of funding in a particular field, or organizations similar to yours that have received grants.

Another foundation document, its federal tax return (Form 990PF), is a vital source of information. Private foundations are required to file this form each year (although inexplicably some don't) with the Internal Revenue Service. They are also required to provide copies, upon request, of these materials.

Form 990s are sometimes available at The Foundation

Center's Cooperating Collections libraries. Several companies also offer them online.

Included on a foundation's 990 Form is the following:

❏ The fair market value of the foundation's assets

❏ Contributions and gifts received by the foundation

❏ Contributions and grants made by the foundation (with a list of grantees as an attachment)

❏ Giving limitations

❏ Names of trustees and foundation officers

❏ Meeting dates or application procedures

◆◆◆

The wealth of directories, periodicals, and research aides available on the subject of foundation funding is testament to the increasingly competitive nature of grant seeking.

With these guides to help you, along with an orderly system of recording information, you should be able to identify any number of top prospects for foundation funding for your organization.

Once you have identified your prospects, it's helpful to devise some system of ranking them, or at least categorizing them as primary prospects or secondary prospects.

When you have completed these steps, you will have a list of foundations -- from among the 55,000 or so in existence today -- whose interests most closely match your organization's needs and are most likely to give you a grant.

Now, you need only to convince them, which the next chapter will show you how to do.

15

Writing
Winning Proposals

Each year, according to the AAFRC Trust for Philanthropy, foundations and corporations contribute $10 to $20 billion to America's nonprofit organizations.

While this doesn't compare to the amount given by individuals — more than $100 billion — it nevertheless confirms the wisdom of having a balanced development program that includes grantseeking.

For the untutored, there are a host of seminars and books on the subject. But in reality, there's no special mystique about proposal writing.

If you have a worthy idea, a solid organization behind you, the time to conduct research, and the ability to communicate in writing, you can prepare a successful proposal.

However, the time-consuming task of writing proposals can be made easier, and more profitable, if you adopt the principles and techniques outlined below.

YOUR PROPOSAL IS ONLY ONE PART

It goes without saying that, to win a grant, you need a persuasively written proposal. But that doesn't mean you should spend all, or even most, of your time on the actual writing.

Grantseeking is a *process*, often an extended one, that also involves planning, research, personal contact, and follow up. What you do before and after writing and submitting your proposal is often more germane than the "i's" you dot or the "t's" you cross.

Consider but one hypothetical. If you had the choice of a personal contact with a high-ranking funding officer *or* a flawlessly written proposal, which would you select? Experienced grantseekers would almost always opt for the former.

Grantseeking isn't grantwriting alone; it is a thorough and thoughtful process and must be viewed in this context.

PRESENT YOURSELF CREDIBLY

While some funders will give to an organization they don't know -- because the project has special appeal -- they nevertheless want to be assured their money is going to a credible organization with strong leadership.

Early in the grantseeking process, therefore, you must view your organization from the perspective of a funder who knows little or nothing about you.

How can you demonstrate to this funder that your cause has merit?

It will demand a great deal of thought -- and articulation -- on your part. You will need to speak confidently about the mission of your organization, the people you serve, the ways you are different from other organizations, the quality of your management, your fiscal record, and the results you have achieved.

This information must be at your fingertips so that as you learn about particular funders, you will know which aspects to stress in your personal contacts and in your proposal.

RESEARCH YOUR POTENTIAL FUNDER

Before writing any proposal, much less submitting it, you need to develop a profile of the funder. This will include:

❑ The funder's stated areas of interest (and recent deviations).

❑ The types and sizes of grants awarded.

❑ Geographical and organizational preferences (and other giving limitations).

❑ Information on application guidelines. And,

❑ A solid grasp of your organization's relationship with the funder, that is, have you received past grants and were the projects successful?

Although harder to uncover, it will also help if you learn how the funder evaluates proposals. Is it by committee or by selected officials? Does your liaison have discretionary power on grants of certain amounts? And do laypeople or trained people in your field review proposals?

SPEAK TO THE FUNDER'S GOALS

The funding source you're approaching has goals of its own. Too often, organizations forget this and concern themselves only with what the grant will do for them and not what it could accomplish for the funder.

But to successfully market your project, you can't emphasize *your* needs and *your* objectives alone. You must look at your project through the funder's eyes and determine how it will further their goals as you understand them.

Ask yourself, What exactly will the funder gain from making this grant? Is it healthier children, better schools, a safer world? Make the case. For even though your organization will carry out the project, the funder will share your achievement.

CALL BEFORE PUTTING PEN TO PAPER

To save yourself a lot of time you should — once you've identified a potential funder and before you've started on any proposal — call them.

You will, among other things, learn if there's a match between you, usually pick up some useful information, and get a sense of whether your project holds any interest for the funder.

Don't be coy over the phone. State why you're calling — to learn more about the funder and to ask if you can submit a proposal — and as briefly as you can describe the project and the amount of money you need.

Further, if you have a president or board member who can present your case persuasively, ask for an appointment. Although they are in the minority, some funders welcome personal visits.

IF YOU GET AN APPOINTMENT

If you are in fact invited to the funder's office, it is a unique opportunity for which you should prepare thoroughly.

First, give thought to who should attend the meeting. Usually it will be the CEO and a board member. But sometimes the project director might attend as well.

Second, research the funder so that your team can demonstrate how the project will further the funder's goals.

Third, make sure each team member has a role to play during the meeting.

Finally, know, before you walk through the door, just what it is you want to accomplish in the meeting.

STYLE AND CONTENT

The reality today is that your proposal will end up in a pile with literally hundreds of others. To have a fighting chance of being read, much less funded, it must be brief, concise, *and* compelling.

But, understand, that's only a start. In addition to being highly readable, your proposal must also demonstrate that:

❑ Your project matches the funder's goals.

❑ Addresses an important need.

❑ You and your staff have the experience to carry out the project.

❑ Yours' is a feasible approach to the problem.

❑ There will be a measurable outcome. And,

❑ You're not duplicating the work of others.

Writing style is important, but don't assume, like rookie proposal writers, that it ever overshadows content.

BLEND LOGIC AND EMOTION

Your proposal must present the facts as you see them, but this doesn't mean it should be devoid of emotion.

In fact, you want to breathe life into your proposal, personalizing it with examples, anecdotes, and illustrations.

Your aim is to *connect*, so that the funder ends up sharing your vision.

To achieve this, take pains to:

❑ Write to a person, not to a funding organization.

❑ Stress the human side, how people's lives will be affected.

❑ Avoid the jargon that's part of the culture of every organization.

❑ Project confidence that the problem can be addressed. And,

❑ Make your points directly, without paragraphs of build-up.

More important than any of these stylistic suggestions, however, is a character issue, namely, integrity.

The goals you cite, the deadlines you set, the budget you present — all of these must be feasible and realistic. If you mislead a funder, not only will your reputation be stained, but word will rapidly spread that your organization is to be avoided.

WRITE, DON'T FRET

As with most challenging tasks, when sitting down to draft a proposal, getting your pen to move can be the hardest part.

You can make the writing easier, however, if you first approach the job in a casual way, jotting down answers to the following questions, without worrying about the flow of your words:

❑ What's an appropriate name for this project?
❑ Why do we need to do it?
❑ What outcome do we hope to see?
❑ What means will we use to achieve the outcome?
❑ Who will be involved?
❑ What makes us qualified?
❑ In what time frame will we operate?
❑ How will we know if we succeed?
❑ How much will it cost?

Often it's best if the person who's most familiar with the project writes the first draft. After all, he or she will usually be its most informed advocate.

If this isn't possible, the development officer can do the job after conferring with that individual.

ORGANIZE YOUR PROPOSAL

The individual components of your proposal will usually

be the following:

A) Cover letter

Considering the sheer volume of proposals submitted, what you write in your cover letter may well determine whether your proposal is considered for review or rejected outright.

This heavy burden makes it imperative that you be clear and succinct. In your cover letter:

• Explain your reasons for approaching this particular funder.

• Outline the contents of your proposal.

• Briefly describe the project.

• State how much you're seeking. And,

• Mention that you'd be happy to meet with the funder and to provide additional information.

Have the chairperson of your board or the CEO sign the letter.

B) Cover page

It may not happen frequently, but it's possible your cover letter will be separated from your proposal.

If this happens, you want the funder still to be able to identify you, so include key information on your cover page such as your name, address, telephone, and contact person.

Moreover, it's always helpful to personalize the cover page by incorporating the name of the funder ("A Proposal to the Halcyon Foundation for...").

C) Table of contents

The table of contents is self-explanatory. It tells your reader what's included in the proposal and the order and page numbers of the items that appear.

For clarity's sake, present the table on one full-page.

D) Abstract

The abstract, or executive summary, distills the key information in your proposal into one or two pages.

Write it after you've completed the rest of the proposal and include a statement of the problem, a description of the project including who will benefit and how, the amount of funding you need, and an explanation of how you will finance the project in the future.

Include as well a brief history of your organization and its mission.

During the initial screening, your abstract may be the only part of your proposal read, so great care should be taken when composing it.

E) Statement of need

Your statement of need tells why your project is necessary.

It presents facts and supporting evidence and attempts to show that your organization grasps the problem and is in a unique position to address it.

Additionally, your statement of need should document: the importance of addressing the problem, not only to the people who will benefit but also to society at large; the need to solve the problem at once; and how solving it matches the goals of the potential funding source.

F) Project description

This section, in which you describe the nuts and bolts of the project, usually has four parts:

• Objectives

Here you describe in detail the measurable outcomes you expect as well as the time frame in which these outcomes will be achieved.

• Methods

In this section, you chronicle the specific activities that will lead to achieving your objectives.

• Staffing and administration

Here you cite the staff, consultants, and volunteers who will be involved and their qualifications and specific roles.

Too, you describe who will manage the project and how

it will be done.

• Evaluation

Here you explain how you will evaluate the project, including the person who will head the evaluation, how results will be reported, and who will receive copies of the evaluation.

G) Organization information

In this section, your aim is to build credibility for your organization. After all, credibility can be more important in securing the grant than your particular project.

Briefly describe how your organization came into being, your mission, and how the proposed project fits within that mission.

Give details on the board and staff and their levels of expertise.

Provide the names and backgrounds of those key to the project.

And, to bolster your case, describe any special facilities or equipment you have to carry out the project.

H) Closing

This section serves as your closing argument, and you should make your case as compellingly as a prosecutor or defense attorney in court would.

Summoning logic *and* emotion, restate what your organization wants to do and why it's important. Paint a picture of the people who will be served, and how they and society as a whole will benefit. Re-emphasize how the project matches the funder's priorities. And, underscore why it must be done now.

I) Budget

Depending on the scope of the project, your budget may take up one page or six pages.

It should outline the total cost of the undertaking and

include items such as personnel costs, rental space, equipment, supplies, insurance, postage, and printing.

Most important is that your budget be realistic and accurately reflect the size of your project.

Here is also the place to explain how you will fund the project once this particular grant ends.

J) Appendices

Include in this section any supporting documents you feel will strengthen your case, or are required by the funder, such as a fact sheet, list of your governing board, case statement, annual report, previous grants received, bio data on project participants, and your IRS tax exemption letter.

Be thorough but don't of course overload the funder with peripheral material.

WHEN ONLY A SIMPLE LETTER IS DESIRED

If yours is a small request, or if the funder discourages full-blown proposals, a simple letter appeal may be appropriate.

The elements of a letter proposal follow the format described here, just in shorter form.

In your three or four page letter, describe your project, the amount of funding you seek, the need for the project, the budget, what you hope to accomplish, and how you will evaluate the outcome.

Include information about your organization and mission, your board of directors, and any pertinent material required by the funder.

PACKAGING YOUR PROPOSAL

Once you've prepared your proposal, you'll want to package it in the most effective way.

Forego any fancy covers or binders (as these will be removed upon arrival anyway), and avoid embossing, gold leaf, and unusual paper.

Keeping your presentation simple and tasteful will impress your potential funder more than any ornate dressings you might apply to it.

FOLLOW UP

Don't put your feet on the desk once you've submitted your proposal. Instead, encourage your contacts to write letters or call or visit any of the funding officials they know.

Further, about two to four weeks after submitting the proposal, call to ask if further information is required. Ask too if you can meet with the funder or arrange for a visit to your organization.

Finally, just before the review meeting, call the funder again to ensure that your materials are complete.

IF YOU RECEIVE A GRANT

If you receive a grant, the obvious first thing to do is to send a thank-you letter (so obvious that many people forget to do it). Have your CEO or board president send out an official acknowledgment.

Second, is to ask the funder if you can publicize the grant. Often the funder encourages publicity but will want to review the text of your release.

Down the line you will be asked to report on the results of your project. While some want updates quarterly, or biannually, most request a final report, several months after the project is completed. It is obviously to your advantage to comply promptly.

IF YOUR PROPOSAL IS DECLINED

If your proposal is rejected, some funders will explain the reasons if you call, especially if you've had personal contact along the way.

Others discourage follow-up calls, a frustrating behavior compounded when the funder's letter doesn't clarify why your project was rejected.

Whatever reaction you receive, work hard to keep the lines of communication open. You will, by doing so, nurture the possibility of future funding.

◆◆◆

Writing is only a part of developing a successful proposal, as this chapter has attempted to show. As important as the words you string together is the orderly, thorough, and thoughtful process that precedes putting pen to paper.

Successful grantseeking is a culminating event and you will enjoy consistent success only if you view it in the total context described here.

16

Attracting Corporate Support

As measured by the number of companies that give to charitable causes and the total dollars contributed, corporate giving has unquestionably risen over the years.

What hasn't increased significantly, however, is the amount companies give as a percentage of their pre-tax profits. This figure perennially hovers around two percent nationally.

This shouldn't be surprising, though, as corporations are in business to make money. Other priorities -- be they stockholders, employee benefits, or equipment purchases -- take precedence and always will.

So while corporate giving may, relatively speaking, be penurious, it nevertheless amounts to billions of dollars each year.

To help you win your fair share of this largesse, the principles, techniques, and strategies of raising corporate money are detailed here.

UNDERSTANDING THE PROCESS

While the principles of winning a corporate gift are similar to attracting a gift from an individual — namely prospect research, articulating a persuasive case, and peer to peer soliciting — there are certain realities of the corporate decision-making process that you must understand.

• *The Liaison*

Most corporations, either formally or informally, have someone (often the public relations or public affairs director) who is responsible for monitoring all requests for support. Usually this person, who serves as the liaison for organizations seeking assistance, has four functions:

❑ To enhance the company's image by supporting particular nonprofit programs.

❑ To match requests for assistance with the objectives of the company.

❑ To decide, in some cases, if your request will be funded.

❑ To evaluate, once a gift is made, how your organization used the money.

Understand, the liaison usually has other responsibilities within the company and will give your proposal only limited attention. Consequently, if you make it easy for him or her, providing all the necessary information, you will greatly enhance your chances for a grant.

• *Contributions Committee*

Most corporations have at least a pro forma contributions committee, usually consisting of the CEO, senior financial officer, and perhaps a public relations officer. Some companies include an employee representative as well.

When reviewing your request, the contributions committee will usually have in mind the following questions:

❑ Will supporting your project enhance our image? Is your project innovative?

❑ Can the results you achieve be evaluated?

❑ Is your organization involved in any controversy?

❑ Are any of our employees actively involved with you?

❑ Have we contributed to you before, and how much?

And, finally,

❑ How much are you asking other corporations to give?

It's rare that you'll be asked to appear before this committee, so your proposal must usually carry the day. It must be diligently prepared, describe the need you plan to meet, your capacity to meet it, and, most important, what benefits the corporation will gain by providing such support.

ASSESSING YOUR CHANCES

The chances of your winning a corporate gift depend on a number of variables, not the least of which is how thoroughly you've examined your own organization as well as your corporate prospect.

To do so, you will need to pay close attention to:

• *The company's areas of interest*

Which of your programs best relate to or match these interests?

• *The economic climate*

Is your corporate prospect prospering at the moment or weathering a downturn?

• *Giving patterns*

Is your prospect on record as supporting your type of program?

• *Your personal contacts*

Do your board members have any connections with key corporate executives?

• *Geography*

Generally speaking, the closer the company to your backyard, the better your chances for a gift.

• *Services rendered to the company*

Do you provide benefits, or potential benefits, to the company's employees?

Once you have assessed these and other factors — which provide a link between you and the company — it is easier to set priorities for contacting each company.

THE RATIONALE FOR CORPORATE GIVING

Generally speaking, companies make charitable contributions for the following reasons:

• *Good corporate citizenship*

Many companies, believing it's smart business, cultivate a positive image in the community

• *Enlightened self-interest*

Since companies hire locally, it's in their interest to help foster an educated and healthy workforce (usually through supporting local colleges, hospitals, and cultural organizations).

• *Key leader(s) interest*

Often a company will support an organization simply because the CEO or other key officials are personally interested. And, finally,

• *Quid pro quo benefits*

As a health agency you provide blood pressure screenings to our employees; as a corporate donor we'll make it worth your while. Voila, a win-win situation.

TYPES OF CORPORATE GIVING

While corporations give through different vehicles (through their philanthropy budget, marketing department, or foundation), they give in only two ways, cash grants and non-cash services and products.

• *Cash*

Because it is the simplest and cleanest, and as most organizations need cash to meet program costs, more than three-quarters of all corporate giving is in the form of cash or "cash equivalents" such as stocks and bonds.

- *Non-cash*

Non-cash giving takes many forms. These include company product donations, equipment donations, land, loaned executives, use of corporate facilities, support of special events, printing services, and low- or no-interest loans.

When approaching a company for the first time, bear in mind it might be easier winning an in-kind gift. This could well be an entree to more significant cash contributions down the line.

ARE YOU READY?

If, with utmost candor, you can answer "yes" to the following questions, you're probably ready to begin approaching corporations:

❑ Can you show that your project is urgent, in need of immediate funding?

❑ Is yours a realistic solution for meeting the need?

❑ Do you and your staff have the qualifications?

❑ Can you measure the results you achieve?

❑ Can your project continue to operate without further support from the corporation? And, finally,

❑ Do you have support documents available, such as your operating budget, an annual report, an IRS tax exemption certificate and the like?

LEADERSHIP

To succeed, on a grand scale, in corporate fund raising, you will need a strong chairperson, typically the chief executive officer of a company that has given or has the capacity to give a significant gift to your organization.

Peer relationships are especially important in the corporate arena, so don't settle for a weak chairperson.

Granted, you may not be able to command the top leadership, but strive for nothing less than the highest level available to you.

Your chairperson's first task will be to form a committee — of peers — who agree to make personal calls. Ideally, solicitations should be one-on-one visits, but group solicitations are also effective in corporate fund raising.

It goes without saying that staff, working with the volunteer, should plan every aspect of the call — who will do the soliciting, what will be covered in the interview, what materials will be needed, and what the follow-up procedure will be.

WHERE TO LOOK FOR PROSPECTS

Almost always, you'll find your best corporate prospects from among the following groupings:

❑ Those that have contributed to you in the past.

❑ Those that are connected to current or former members of your board.

❑ Those where you have friends (alumni, former employees, colleagues with clout) in highly placed positions.

❑ Those located in the same community or region as you.

❑ Those whose employees benefit directly from your services.

❑ Those national corporations with formal giving programs that mirror the interests of your organization.

UNCOVERING CORPORATE DATA

Corporations, except for the very large, generally don't publish information about their contributions program. Information about their priorities, application procedures, type and number of grants, amounts — this is all obtained slowly, mostly from direct experience, and usually through leaders or volunteers with a link to the company.

Of course, print and online directories published by *Dun & Bradstreet, Moody's, Standard & Poor's,* as well as *Who's Who* should prove helpful as well.

While it can be a painstaking process, at least your research is limited, as only companies with plants and offices in your region or service area, and with whom you have some linkage, should receive your attention.

Focus your research on the following groups of companies:

❑ Those with which your board members are affiliated (directly or indirectly).

❑ Those with employees who use, or can use, your services.

❑ Those where your donors are employed or with whom they're connected.

❑ Those from which your organization buys products and services.

❑ Those having services or products that match your interests and which could gain from investing in your future.

As to specific information you will need, gather the following data on each serious prospect:

• Full name and correct address of company
• Corporate assets
• Type of business
• List of corporate officers and directors of corporate foundation if any, and a list of its officers
• Sales volume
• Previous giving history
• Decision-making procedure
• Gifts to other organizations
• Connections with your organization
• History of your dealings with the corporation

- Local subsidiaries and officers
- Corporate gift-committee names, connections, and shared interests

Because there must be a logical reason for a company to consider making a gift to you, it's safe to assume that you can't know too much about your prospects.

LEAD CORPORATE GIFTS

When it comes to charitable contributions, corporations pay close attention to what their competition is doing. You can leverage this to your advantage by approaching your community's dominant prospect first. Other corporations will, you can bet, gauge their contribution by what the leader does.

CULTIVATING KEY OFFICIALS

Typically, organizations give little thought to cultivating corporate prospects until the subject of fund raising comes up. But if you really hope to attract corporate money, you must make corporate decision-makers familiar with your work. In fact, you must guide them through the same thought processes which originally led your board members to become involved. *Ongoing* cultivation should involve any and all of the following:

❑ Sending your organization's newsletter, campaign updates, or feature articles to corporate liaisons.

❑ Paying a "cultivation call" on these representatives to introduce yourself and get general information.

❑ Involving the company's officers and employees in your work, asking them to participate in associate programs, planning sessions, advisory groups, or to serve on an appropriate committee.

❑ Inviting corporate officers to be your guests at special events.

The more involved you can get the liaison, the greater your chances of getting funded.

CAREFULLY CRAFTED PROPOSALS

Presenting a thoughtful, well-written proposal *tailored to your prospect's needs* is absolutely essential.

Only such a proposal can hope to compete and gain an edge over the hundreds of others spilling across the liaison's desk. An effective proposal will:

❑ Be a concise statement of your organization's impact on the people you serve and on the community.

❑ Document how your work affects the corporation, its employees, their families, and other constituencies.

❑ Show how the company will benefit from making such a gift. And,

❑ Demonstrate how your organization will accomplish its objectives with the financial support.

In other words you must, as you would with any individual prospect, articulate a persuasive case for support. And don't overdo it with written materials. Your proposal — and often it's a simple two-page letter — should contain the information a corporation needs to make a decision, and no more. Write it in a way that's easy to read, to the point, upbeat, and devoid of jargon.

Accompany your proposal with a board of directors list, proof of tax-exempt status, audited financial statements, and other appendices requested by the company.

MAKING THE CONTACT

Ironically, the one phase of corporate fund raising requiring the least amount of time is the actual solicitation, though of course it remains the most critical. This is simply because most of the groundwork, that is, research and cultivation, has taken place prior to the ask.

In corporate fund raising, just as in individual fund raising, principles of peer solicitation prevail. And it is extremely important, if at all possible, to make the initial corporate contact through a social or business peer. Granted, the gift will come from the corporate treasury, but the solicitation is still personal and success may well depend upon the position of the solicitor and the respect he or she commands.

What if your organization's relationship with a corporation is less personal? It is still possible to secure corporate support, though it's likely be harder to get major support. A brief visit by the development director and a key volunteer board member with the corporate liaison can lead to valuable information about how and when to approach the corporation, the size of gift to request, and the features of your program to stress.

If neither a personal solicitation nor friendly visit is possible, you'll have to rely more on your cultivation of the prospect and your written proposal.

POST-DECISION FOLLOW-UP
In the end, your proposal will either trigger support (though not necessarily the amount you sought) or it will be declined, in which case it's perfectly appropriate to ask how this decision was reached and whether a modified proposal can be submitted.

Regardless of the outcome, it's wise to immediately thank the company and its representatives for reviewing your proposal. A gracious response to rejection may in fact help lead to future funding.

If you are successful in securing a gift, you will want to express the same gratitude you would for an individual donor. A personal letter from your president and perhaps your executive director, as well as recognition plaques, certificates, and other mementos are all appropriate.

As for public recognition, you will need to clear this with the company. Some will seek the exposure while others may want anonymity, fearing a deluge of similar requests for support.

One last word: don't forget your new-found friends. Continue your contact with the company. Give your liaison periodic reports on how the money is being spent, send a copy of your annual report, invite key officials to appropriate events - all of which will enhance your chance for ongoing corporate support.

◆◆◆

While they will always be consumed by other priorities, corporation officials, by and large, do see the need for contributing to their community. But seldom will they take the lead.

The onus is and always will be on you to dramatize the need, explain how you are especially equipped to address it, and show how the corporation will benefit by helping you financially. If you can accomplish these mighty objectives, there are tremendous opportunities for creative collaboration between you and corporate America.

17

Planned Giving

Today, people over the age of 60 hold most of America's wealth. Not for much longer, though, as baby boomers are poised to inherit their parents' assets.

The enormous transfer of wealth that will occur over the next several years will create unheard of potential for the field of development.

This is particularly true in the area of planned giving, where gift options such as income trusts, annuities, bequests, and life insurance will increasingly be seen as attractive ways to 1) ensure current income, 2) generate tax advantages, and 3) provide for charitable organizations.

If you do not have a planned giving program in place, the following 12 steps will illustrate what you need to do right now to prepare you for the opportunities in store.

MAKE SURE YOU'RE READY

While it's simple enough to start a bequest society, launching a full-scale planned giving program requires a good deal of organizational self-examination.

Among the internal questions you, your board, and staff will have to address are the following:

❑ Does your organization have a record of accomplishments?

❑ What is the history of your fund raising activities?

❑ Do you currently have a base of annual donors?

❑ Have you ever had a major gifts campaign?

❑ Do you have the constituency to justify life income trusts and other complex gift vehicles?

❑ Do you have the resources to finance a planned giving program?

❑ Has your board been actively involved in your fund raising and can you expect them to make a planned gift?

❑ Can you and your board accept that revenue won't be realized from your program for at least three to five years?

Many organizations, especially newer ones, seek immediate, outright contributions. That makes sense. But for many other organizations, not to actively seek planned gifts is short-sighted and very costly in the long run.

PUT A SPECIALIST IN CHARGE

If your planned giving program is to take wings, you will need someone who can:

1) Develop a comprehensive, long-term plan.

2) Make it his or her job to understand the full range of gift options.

3) Use that knowledge to identify and attract support. And,

4) Spend a significant amount of time visiting prospects.

As should be evident by the time commitment required, this is neither the job of a volunteer nor your organization's attorney. A member of your development staff must be in charge.

Understand, that individual needn't be a tax expert, but he or she must have -- or be willing to develop -- a working knowledge of the laws affecting charitable giving *and* the administrative ability to process gift agreements.

Volunteers do have a role to play in planned giving; they can be especially effective in introducing prospects to your organization and nurturing the relationships. But the pivotal person remains the staff specialist. It is to him or her your volunteers will turn for technical expertise.

FORM A PLANNED GIVING COMMITTEE

Often a standing committee of the board, the charge of this group is to formulate policies for your program, help in its promotion, assist in identifying prospects, and generally oversee the direction of your program.

You'll want at least one attorney, one accountant, and perhaps a bank trust officer on board. But don't overload the committee with financial professionals. Include as well some community leaders, maybe a past member of your board, and some standout volunteers from your annual or capital campaigns.

The aim is to have financially skilled people who can provide technical expertise, and lay members who will exercise sound judgment on the needs of your organization. Hopefully both groups know appropriate prospects in the community.

Keep in mind that, wealthy or not, all committee members should make a financial commitment. The options in planned giving, from simple bequests, to gifts of life insurance, to pooled income gifts, make it possible for practically everyone to participate.

ORGANIZE AN ADVISORY COMMITTEE

Distinguished from your planned giving committee, the primary purpose of this group, composed almost exclusively of attorneys, trust officers, estate planners, certified financial planners, realtors, and chartered life underwriters, is to provide advice and counsel on the technical aspects of your program.

Chosen properly, this committee can be instrumental in other ways as well -- giving visibility to your program, identifying major prospects, assisting in solicitations, and participating in estate planning seminars to name but a few.

ESTABLISH YOUR POLICIES

Before you can launch your program, your planned giving committee must develop and submit a set of policies for the board's approval.

The items usually presented to the board include the following:

1) The reasons you're establishing the planned giving program.

2) A description of the types of gifts (i.e. bequests, pooled income funds, trusts) you will be seeking.

3) Investment procedures you'll follow.

4) A statement outlining the general purposes of your program.

5) A list of those who will be authorized to negotiate planned gifts.

6) Permission to form a planned gifts advisory committee.

7) The name of the legal counsel you wish to retain.

The vast majority of gifts will fall comfortably within established guidelines and be handled at the staff level. For the few cases involving special risks, the planned giving committee and the board will have to be consulted.

RETAIN COMPETENT COUNSEL

Even though you have a planned giving committee and an advisory committee, you'll still need to retain legal counsel for the "down and dirty" work. There is, after all, a limit to the amount of work volunteer committees can do. You cannot, for instance, expect them to prepare wills or draft charitable remainder trusts.

You must have an experienced attorney not only to provide general counsel and advice but also to:

❏ Keep you current on tax law changes.

❏ Review your promotional materials for accuracy.

❏ Draft sample wills and trusts.

❏ Represent you in probate proceedings.

❏ Negotiate directly with your donor's attorney. And,

❏ Meet with donors as required.

Is it wise to use the attorney already retained by your organization?

Not usually. Whereas he or she may be familiar with a range of issues, including employee benefit plans, insurance, and personnel matters, it's unlikely the person has extensive knowledge about charitable giving tax laws.

ESTABLISH YOUR BUDGET

Funding a full-fledged planned giving program, especially in the start-up phase, is not inexpensive.

Among the items you'll need to budget for are: travel, professional development, materials, software, outside administration fees, reference materials, postage, office space, legal fees, and general office support. Then too, there are the salary requirements of the person who's going to head up the program.

Factors such as the location and size of your constituency, as well as the cultivation activities you plan, will dictate your specific budgetary needs.

But make no mistake. Planned giving requires a long-term investment of staff time and funds. Unless you can budget your program for five years - the period it normally takes to begin seeing a return - it's best to delay your program rather than launch it on a shoestring.

DEVELOP YOUR MATERIALS

Your marketing communications, at least in the beginning, will be targeted to your current donors, educating them about the basics of planned giving.

You'll find it useful to have a series of brochures at your disposal.

The first, an adaptation of your organization's case statement, describes your mission, goals, and the people who benefit from your work.

The second outlines the general methods people can use to make a planned gift, and the benefits accruing to the donor.

The remaining brochures are each devoted to a single giving method (i.e. bequests, trusts, annuities, and life insurance) and are sent to individuals who have expressed an interest in your program.

You can, with legal counsel, develop your own materials or purchase them from various companies and have them imprinted with your organization's name and logo.

COMPILE A PROSPECT LIST

Just as in capital campaigns -- and in all forms of fund raising really -- your best prospects for a planned gift are those closest to your organization: namely, your board of directors and current donors.

If you announce your program by writing to these supporters and asking whether they've included your organization in their will or would like information about making a planned gift, you'll find that many of them will respond favorably.

From this core group you then reach out to other, less likely, prospects: the people you serve, those who regularly use your services or attend your organization's activities, even lapsed contributors. But keep in mind that your program will succeed only if you market it to those having some link to you already.

While there isn't a typical planned giving donor per se -- almost anyone can participate in one gift vehicle or another -- generally speaking, your prospects will be older, have some wealth, and be without children. Then too, surviving spouses sometimes wish to honor the wishes of a wife or husband who played a role in your organization.

One final note. Only contact as many prospects as you can follow up with in a reasonable time, say 48 hours. Each inquiry you receive deserves prompt attention.

BEGIN CULTIVATION VISITS

At the heart of every successful planned giving program is personal contact with prospects.

Through your mailings, seminars and various cultivation activities, you'll identify people who request a personal visit.

Unlike calls upon annual or capital campaign prospects -- where the person is actually asked for a gift -- your initial visit with a planned giving prospect is usually to build a personal relationship and to learn about his or her interests, needs, and financial situation.

It takes months if not years to get to the actual asking stage.

Still, your success will to a good degree depend on the number of visits you make, your ability to focus on the needs of the donor, and your patience in building the relationship.

ASK FOR THE GIFT

The time will come, when your prospects are sufficiently cultivated, to ask for a gift.

If you've nurtured the relationship, your prospect will likely feel like a friend -- and you may be tempted to delay asking or feel awkward about bringing up the subject of money.

But, remember, you are sitting across from this person only because your organization hired you to raise money; and you must keep your ultimate goal in mind.

At the same time, your prospect's needs must remain primary:

1) She must have enough money to provide for herself and her family, now and for the future.

2) She should first make provisions to her natural heirs and to others for whom she feels a responsibility.

It is your duty, as development officer, to protect the donor from giving away money he or she cannot afford, and to ensure that no agreement is signed that benefits your organization at the expense of the donor.

KEEP YOUR PROGRAM RUNNING

Securing a planned gift is often a lengthy process.

Not only is a series of visits with each prospect required -- for a gift you may not receive for 10 years - but several factors converge to make the process quite slow:

❏ People seldom like to think about their deaths.

❏ The amounts of money involved are usually large.

❏ By their very nature, planned gifts are often complicated to arrange.

❏ Even when a prospect decides to give, there are legal documents to prepare, review, and revise.

With many fund raising activities, you can measure their success on a cost-to-benefit ratio: you spend this amount of money and get this much in return. But planned giving doesn't offer this convenient barometer, as it usually takes three to five years to see a return.

In the meantime, your organization must continue to fund the program on faith that it will produce results. For many chief executives and board members that requires foresight, not to mention a great deal of patience.

◆◆◆

Planned giving has long been the neglected child in development efforts, and it's easy to understand why.

Given the technical nature of the field, the high start-up costs, the need for a specialist, not to mention the slow pay-off, it's tempting to let a bequest blurb in your newsletter be the sum and total of your program.

But such an approach will be costly in terms of lost support -- much of which will wend its way to other organizations with steelier determination.

18

Working with Consultants

If a personal problem is troubling you, one for which you need advice and a fresh perspective, there are various places to turn: a friend, colleague, cleric, neighbor, even a therapist.

By the same token, when an organization has a problem, or has reached an impasse, or is lacking in expertise, a common place to turn is a consultant.

Fortunately, when the help you seek pertains to fund raising, there are hundreds if not thousands of consultants providing a wide range of annual, capital, endowment, and planned giving services.

But consultants are no different than lawyers, doctors, tax accountants, or shoe cobblers. Some are terrific, others are terrible.

To help you find the right consultant, negotiate a fair and equitable agreement, and begin your relationship on a productive note, the following 14 guidelines are offered.

WHAT A CONSULTANT DOES

Fund raising consultants perform a myriad of tasks, but most commonly they're called upon to:

❑ Conduct a feasibility study.

❑ Prepare your campaign case and other materials.

❑ Provide full-time (resident) campaign management.

❑ Provide part-time counseling.

In whatever capacity you use your consultant, he or she should be able to:

1) Gauge your fund raising potential.

2) Tell you whether your organization is ready to launch a successful drive and, if not, what you need to do to lay the foundation.

3) Develop a comprehensive fund raising plan, with techniques and approaches tailored to your organization.

4) Provide continuing direction by ensuring that campaign plans are acted upon, deadlines are met, volunteers are trained, and revisions take place when needed. And,

5) Offer, or have access to, communications help in the form of graphic design, copywriting, audiovisual presentations.

DISPENSING WITH SOME MYTHS

Of the misconceptions that surround the role of consultants, the most widely held seem to be the following:

• *A consultant will solicit for you.*

By and large, consultants do *not* raise money directly -- that is, they will *not* solicit for you. Their role is to steer, oversee, train, monitor, even goad your board and staff to raise money using proven principles and techniques.

• *A consultant will relieve you and your board of responsibility for fund raising.*

To the contrary, a consultant will clarify — and more often than not expand — the role volunteers and staff play in fund raising. Rather than take over your fund raising, he or she will insist that all key players participate fully.

• *A consultant will bring in prospects for you to solicit.*

Your board members must already know, or have some connection or entree to, your prospects. Such linkage is the sine qua non of successful fund raising. A consultant may occasionally identify someone new, but this happens rarely.

• *A consultant will provide the magic formula.*

In a way this is true. He or she will demonstrate techniques that work, avoid mistakes, and ensure that the right things happen at the right time. This truly is a magic formula of sorts.

ADVANTAGES AND DISADVANTAGES

As with most aspects of life, there are advantages and disadvantages to hiring consultants.

• Advantages

A consultant brings objectivity to your organization and enables you to see problems you're too close to see.

A consultant, as the paid expert, has credibility, allowing him or her to garner support for actions and approaches that might not be heeded if they came from staff.

A consultant can insist that fundamentals and proper sequences be followed, something very important when antsy board members threaten to prematurely approach your top prospects.

A consultant can provide unsurpassed training to your staff in effective fund raising techniques and practices.

• Disadvantages

While it may in fact be cost effective, using a consultant can still be expensive up front.

Because a consultant will direct you in raising money, but not raise it for you, he or she may provide limited operational help, something you may need as much, if not more than, strategic guidance.

If you use a large consulting firm, the person who best matches your needs and has the right chemistry may not be available.

DETERMINING YOUR NEEDS

Your first step in hiring a consultant is to know exactly what *you* want for your organization and what you desire from the consultant. The more specific you can be, the easier it will be to identify the help you need.

❑ Do you need a feasibility study? A consultant can conduct interviews, sift through the data, and make recommendations.

❑ Do you need your development program audited? A consultant can analyze your staff, board, methodology, procedures, and recommend steps to strengthen your program.

❑ Do you need advice, someone on whom to test your ideas? A consultant can fill this need, giving advice and offering a brand of candor staff cannot.

❑ Does your board need fund raising training? A consultant can be most helpful here. Or,

❑ Do you need a consultant for that most familiar of assignments, campaign management? Here, a consultant can offer very specific advice on annual, capital, or endowment drives.

Having a solid grasp on what you need and what you can afford to spend will make the process of finding a consultant easier and less frustrating.

CREATING A LIST OF CANDIDATES

Probably the best way to identify appropriate consultants to interview is to check with development officers at organizations similar to yours to learn which ones they have used. In building your list of candidates, keep the following factors in mind:

- *Size of company*

Do you want a full-service firm with a range of in-house capabilities such as copywriters and graphic designers, or would a small company or even an independent consultant serve you equally well?

- *Working style*

Would your board and CEO mesh better with a buttoned-down firm or one a bit more casual?

- *Type of experience*

Is your organization so unique that you need a consultant who's had experience with causes like yours or would a skilled generalist do?

- *Belief in your cause*

Do you want someone who has empathy for your cause or, for example, is of the same religious faith. A belief in your cause won't usually affect a consultant's quality of work, but your board may desire the extra connection.

THE INTERVIEW PROCESS

You will want to recruit a group of interested board members and staff to participate in the hiring of a consultant. This group should be made up of your board president, the development committee chair, your organization's CEO, and key members of your fund raising staff.

Next, develop a short list of questions to ask all of your candidates about their services, fees, and staffing. Finally, determine which committee member will lead the discussion.

Emphasize to this person, and to the committee as a whole, that it's vital to keep the focus of the discussion on the consultant and his or her services, not on your organization and its needs.

You will, during these interviews, be trying to answer the

following questions:

❑ Will this consultant, and his or her style, fit well with our board, CEO, and donors?

❑ Will the individual command our respect and be able to direct us?

❑ Does the consultant have sufficient experience so that we'll have faith in his or her recommendations?

❑ Does the consultant seem flexible, that is, will he or she react constructively when and if our strategy and goals change?

❑ What will this consulting relationship cost, including direct and out-of-pocket expenses?

Two caveats: If you hire a large firm, be sure you know who will be assigned to you and interview that person.

Secondly, don't expect your candidates to offer recommendations at the interview. A seasoned pro will immerse himself or herself in your organization before suggesting courses of action.

CHEMISTRY MATTERS

If during the interview you don't feel comfortable with the consultant, whether it's his or her general attitude or appearance or demeanor, go with your instinct and move along to your next candidate.

When the pressure of your campaign mounts, you will need to have confidence in your consultant and if this is lacking from the outset it's not likely to surface later.

Your relationship must be one of mutual faith and respect; and it will be productive only to the extent that it is.

WHEN CHECKING REFERENCES

Needless to say, you'll want to contact present and former clients of the candidate you're considering.

When checking references, you'll find it more fruitful to ask specific questions rather than seek a general evaluation of the consultant. Some of the more important questions you want answered include:

❑ All things considered, would you hire this consultant again?

❑ Was the consultant dependable, punctual for meetings, and did he or she promptly return your phone calls?

❑ Was the consultant able to relate effectively with you and your board?

❑ Do you feel you got your money's worth?

❑ Were your needs and problems grasped quickly by the consultant?

❑ Was the work you contracted for completed on schedule?

❑ When changes to your plan occurred, were there any problems with renegotiation?

❑ Did your staff respect the consultant and were they able to work with him or her?

Finally, describe the problem your organization faces and ask if the consultant in question would be right for the job.

WHO HIRES IS CRITICAL

A consultant cannot be forced upon an organization; your board and CEO must genuinely want his or her services if there's to be a solid chance for success.

Those who will be working most closely with the consultant should be the ones to make the final hiring decision. For example, if your consultant will work primarily with your board members, then key trustees should participate in the interviewing and make the selection.

If, on the other hand, the consultant will work principally with the development director, then that person should have the power to decide.

FEES

Consultant fees are extremely varied. Some who charge premium rates are excellent, others are mediocre. The same is true for those charging low fees. (In and of themselves, fees aren't as reliable an indicator of ability as how far in advance your candidate is booked -- good consultants often aren't available to you for several months.)

Your agreement with the consultant should specify both fixed fees and budgeted expenses such as clerical help, office space, telephone charges and the like. Any agreement should of course be in writing.

You can arrange payment in one of three ways:

❑ You pay the consultant a fixed sum at regular intervals -- usually monthly;

❑ You pay for each task or component of your project as it's completed;

❑ You pay a lump sum at the end (an arrangement not often agreed to by consultants).

Whether consultants should be paid a flat fee, commission, or percentage is a matter constantly debated. There is no easy answer, other than to let ethics guide your decision.

NEGOTIATING A CONTRACT

When formulating a contract with your consultant, it's important to clearly define your proposed relationship, outlining the following:

❑ The specific tasks your consultant will perform -- the period when work begins and ends.

❑ If you're using a large firm, which representative will be working with you.

❑ A clause allowing you and the consultant to terminate the contract, with notice of usually 30 days.

❑ Specifics on who will own such items as original art, mailing lists, interview data.

❑ The procedure for approving written materials -- the total the consultant will be paid, and when, as well as information about out of pocket costs.

It goes without saying that your organization's attorney should review the contract before it is signed.

The more effort put into formalizing your agreement, the less you may have to spend later if disagreements arise.

RESPECT NOT AFFECTION

To be sure, a good consultant is a positive force, but he or she must be perfectly frank even if that's interpreted as unduly negative.

If your organization isn't ready for a campaign, an experienced consultant won't hesitate to tell your governing board so. If some impatient trustees want to leapfrog the process and solicit prospects before they're cultivated, a good consultant will restrain them.

When these and other tensions arise, your consulting .relationship may indeed be uncomfortable, as well it should be since your consultant's role is to ask hard questions, force you to address emotion-laden issues, push you to reach deadlines, and challenge you to do your best.

You and your board may not find the consultant personable and friendly, which is fine. It is only important that you professionally respect him or her.

TRUST THE CONSULTANT

Once you've rigorously interviewed a consultant, checked out references, and signed a contract, don't spend valuable time second-guessing the person; don't conjure up reasons for why something he or she has suggested won't work; and don't talk about how you've tried something similar and it didn't work.

Trust the consultant, his knowledge, and his experience. After all, that's why you hired him or her in the first place.

EVALUATION

Once your project is completed and your consultant has moved on, you must address that all important question: For what your organization received, was the consultant worth the price?

To answer this, you'll need to examine three factors: how well *you* fulfilled your role; how well the consultant accomplished his or hers; and whether your organization has progressed as a result of the relationship.

Among the questions you'll need to ask are the following:

❑ Did your board and CEO fully commit to working with the consultant?

❑ Were your objectives clear from the beginning?

❑ Did you have an adequate budget to work with?

❑ Did the consultant present a sound plan and was it followed?

❑ Were the appropriate people in your organization available to the consultant?

❑ When asked for information, did you provide it promptly to the consultant?

❑ Did your CEO and board respect the consultant?

❑ Was the consultant able to adapt to changing circumstances and still keep sight of your overall goal?

❑ Were you, at the conclusion of your relationship, left with any models or systems that can be continued by your board and staff?

❑ Did the consultant accomplish what he or she was hired to do?

And finally, as a result of the consultant's work, were your organization's goals and objectives significantly advanced?

◆◆◆

When all is said and done, your consulting relationship will have a great chance of succeeding if you follow three simple steps:

1) Be sure your organization's key leadership actively works with the consultant. All activities must be cooperative ones. Your board simply can't turn everything over to the expert.

2) Keep the channels of communication open. You must be in constant touch with your consultant about the current status of your project, upcoming activities, problems encountered, and successes and disappointments to date.

3) Respect the professional you hired. Presumably, you selected your particular consultant because of the knowledge and skill he or she demonstrated. Remember that after you've signed the contract. You don't have to always agree but it's critical you respect your consultant's professional judgment.

19

Fund Raising on the Internet

Gary Grobman, an authority on the Internet and author of The Nonprofit Organization's Guide to E-Commerce and co-author of The Non-Profit Internet Handbook contributed this and the following chapter.

It has been nothing short of a communications revolution.

Fundraisers are using the Internet to reach out to find new donors, identify promising sources for foundation and government grants, and partner with third party providers to raise funds for their organizations.

What makes Internet fundraising so attractive is that it slashes the transaction costs involved in both generating a new contribution and encouraging repeat giving. And it saves considerable time as well.

If you're not taking advantage of what the 'Net offers fundraisers, you're missing out on tapping a source of funds that was, at best, remotely available just a few short years ago.

ADVANTAGES OF INTERNET FUNDRAISING

Using the Internet isn't likely to replace traditional fundraising techniques any time soon. Philanthropy depends on a human, face-to-face connection.

What the Internet does provide, however, is another arrow in the quiver — offering powerful advantages over traditional fundraising, such as:

• *Donors find you rather than the other way around.*

By use of search engines, directories, Web rings, and links from other Web sites, potential donors will find your organization even if you don't have an effective strategy for reaching out to them.

• *There's almost universal access and increasing comfort with online transactions.*

Even those without their own computers have access to the Internet through their local libraries, and free e-mail accounts are available to anyone with the motivation to sign up.

People who only a few years ago didn't have an e-mail account eagerly participate in E-Bay auctions, purchase airline tickets and hotel rooms online, buy and sell securities, and examine PDF-format 990s online before considering a contribution.

• *There is 24/7, global access and availability.*

Donors have the opportunity to initiate contact with your organization 24 hours a day, seven days a week, and make an instant contribution.

There are no postage or long distance charges (donors don't even have to know the address or telephone number of your organization). Rather than having to write a check, find an envelope and stamp, and mail their gifts, donors can get the instant gratification they seek, anytime of the day or night by making their contribution via credit card or electronic cash payment, and having it acknowledged immediately by automated e-mail response.

This encourages impulse giving, which is particularly effective during off-hours when no one is staffing the telephones of the organization.

• *In most cases, there are lower costs compared to traditional fundraising methods.*

Solicitation materials can be modified electronically at any time at little or no cost, with no extra charges for color. Compare this to printing full-color, glossy brochures that are costly to update and are often thrown away without having been read.

While printing technology has improved, it'll be quite some time before someone figures out how to incorporate the animations, scrolling messages, and flashing screens that make Web pages more dynamic than their print counterparts.

• *There is increased donor receptivity to soliciting via the Internet.*

Your fundraising message can be delivered by e-mail and read at a time that's convenient for the reader. Compare this to expensive and time-consuming direct mail and telephone solicitation appeals, which, more often than not, annoy and alienate rather than build a positive relationship with your donor.

• *Internet fundraising can be easily integrated with other marketing and promotional materials and programs.*

Solicitations can be coordinated with other features of

your organization's Web site, such as being included in an electronic newsletter, posted on donor recognition Web pages, on links to your organization's sales of goods and services (see next chapter), and testimonials about your work that indirectly enhance opportunities for giving.

• *There are decreased transaction costs for Internet-based gift processing and donor outreach efforts.*

New business models make it easier to partner with third parties to streamline the online giving process and reach donors who otherwise might never have heard of your organization. Computers using sophisticated software automate many processes, such as accounting, database management, and donor acknowledgment, that previously relied on time-consuming work by staff.

• *There are increased opportunities to build positive relationships with the business community.*

Many for-profit businesses are willing to sponsor the Web sites of charities, usually with no more than a "thank you" or a link (typically in the form of the sponsor's logo) from your site to that sponsor's own Web site.

DISADVANTAGES OF ONLINE FUNDRAISING

As you know, nothing's perfect and using the Internet for fundraising does have its disadvantages as well:

• *The online medium can be impersonal compared to face-to-face fundraising.*

Online fundraising, with rare exceptions — such as when using real-time conferencing — isn't face-to-face. The personal, human contact, with the ability to read, interpret, and respond to body language and other non-text cues, is an important component of fundraising, particularly when soliciting large gifts. There are limitations in relying on only what can be viewed on a computer screen to communicate.

• *The regulatory climate remains murky.*

There are myriad unresolved legal and regulatory issues that are surfacing as a result of online fundraising. Among them are the degree to which states regulate it, and what the roles are of third party for-profit companies that agree to serve as an intermediary between donors and an organization.

• *There are vulnerabilities as a result of having to rely on for-profit third parties.*

Many charitable organizations are unwilling or unable to build the infrastructure to seek and process online gifts. For-profit providers have sprung up to offer their services. Many have no track record for reliability, ethical conduct, or financial stability. In addition, new business models have been created that involve partnerships and affiliation agreements with for-profits.

The need for clear agreements between charitable organizations and these third parties raises issues of transaction costs, issues of motivation, opportunities for outright fraud, privacy with respect to sensitive donor data, and the potential inability of an organization to control a third party's use of their logo. Abuse by third party providers in the name of an organization can stain a reputation that took years to build.

TECHNIQUES

Despite the disadvantages, in almost every case the advantages of using the Internet to supplement traditional fundraising far outweigh the disadvantages.

Almost every major charitable organization in the U.S. has reported raising significant revenues utilizing the Internet. Among the techniques organizations are using to harness the power of the Internet for fundraising are:

1. Using e-mail to communicate organizational needs to stakeholders.

While the "culture" of participation in the Internet community is still evolving, it is clear that an organization sending an unsolicited message to a list of 10 million rented e-mail addresses is violating the spirit of the online culture.

The consequences of sending "spam" solicitations range from a revocation of Internet access by your organization's service provider, to getting a response filled with "flame" messages (threatening or otherwise nasty e-mails), to damaging your reputation and alienating potential donors and other stakeholders.

What is less clear is what types of e-mail solicitation are acceptable, and what types are the most effective. Communicating organizational needs by e-mail to stakeholders who already have some relationship to the organization, such as donors, board members, and those served by the organization, is usually appropriate.

2. Using the organization's Web site to solicit donations.

Among ways this is done is to place a "donate here" link on the home page. Clicking on the button links the donor to a secure page (i.e., where the information sent by the donor is encrypted). The page will have an online form permitting the donor to make an online contribution by credit card.

Typically it will also have information about other methods for giving, such as a form that can be mailed or faxed to the organization, a telephone number to call during business hours, and information about planned giving. It may also have an offer for a modest "thank you" gift for donors, such as a mug with the organization's logo, a calendar, or a t-shirt.

3. Incorporating into the organization's Web site features that promote online giving.

Among examples are electronic newsletters that can be subscribed to for free from the organization's home page. The newsletter is periodically sent as e-mail to subscribers, providing news about the organization's activities and programs — and perhaps a subtle appeal somewhere in the text for funds for a specific program or purpose.

Charitable organizations have discovered that building an online community using their Web site promotes fundraising. Such a site encourages repeat visits by offering a chat room, a message board, volunteer site, opportunities for feedback — such as in the form of online surveys — and content that is updated on a regular basis.

4. Putting together an online auction.

With only a modest investment, substantial funds can be raised by offering goods and services to the public using online auction software, or using the services of a provider that administers online auctions.

Charitable organizations can often obtain items, such as donated artifacts from celebrities, that are valuable to millions who may never have heard of the organization or may not care about its mission. They will make a bid because of their interest in the items themselves. (see next chapter).

5. Collaborating with a provider that can help your organization raise funds online.

Some organizations are partnering with for-profit providers that engage in creative business models that generates charitable contributions.

For example, "click-to-give" sites reward visitors who click on a link to a sponsoring business by making a modest gift to a designated charity. On other sites, individuals that agree to install special software on their computer to keep track of online retail purchases can designate a portion of the sale price to a participating organization. Another model allows online supermarket coupon bar codes to be printed out that let shoppers make a contribution in the amount of the coupon, with the gift charged at the checkout line, aggregated, and sent to the charitable organization.

CONCLUSION

The Internet offers so many advantages that the primary advice offered here consists of three words: Go for it! But keep in mind that traditional fundraising strategies shouldn't be neglected, even if they're unexciting by comparison. Online fundraising is just another option, and it will likely be many years before organizations find that the bulk of their gifts comes from the Internet.

20

Nonprofit E-Commerce

Gary Grobman, an authority on the Internet and author of The Nonprofit Organization's Guide to E-Commerce and co-author of The Non-Profit Internet Handbook contributed this and the previous chapter.

To a mayfly, twenty-four hours is a lifetime. To a species, a million years may be the blink of an eye. And to nonprofit technology, a few years seems like an eternity.

The velocity of change is already at warp speed, and is accelerating. It seems like only yesterday that nonprofits were using typewriters to bang out letters, one at a time, to raise money.

Today, these same organizations can turn to a spectrum of sophisticated tools and techniques to reach out to their intended audience — whether to solicit funds, identify grant sources, or sell goods and services to increase their revenues. This chapter focuses on the latter endeavor — how nonprofits can use the Internet to sell goods and services.

ADVANTAGES OF E-COMMERCE

Once you overcome (or at least manage) the hurdles of generating revenues via the Internet, the benefits are staggering:

• Your store is open seven days a week, 24 hours a day, and there's always free parking.

• Your Web site is only a click away from millions of potential customers and donors world-wide.

• Most of your online store's operations can be automated using customized or off-the-rack software, and the dull, repetitive tasks of order fulfillment, payment processing, gift acknowledgment, and marketing can be performed by this software, or by third parties, for reasonable fees.

• You can harness the strength of sophisticated online search engines, directories, Web rings, electronic mailing lists, and online communities to help potential customers find you and the products and services you offer.

DISADVANTAGES OF E-COMMERCE

There are, of course, serious disadvantages to using the Internet to expand the reach of your organization's marketing of goods and services. Among the most important are:

• *Customer service*
Some purchasers won't receive their orders, or orders will be delayed. Or they'll want to know how to return an item, and what their options are for exchanges. They'll call you, and you need policies in place to address typical concerns — which should be displayed on your store's Web site. Sales made to those in another country present an additional layer of problems to be resolved.

• *Financial management*
You will need a system to print invoices, collect and remit

taxes (including state sales taxes and federal unrelated business income taxes), and verify and process payments.

• *Security*

You will need encryption software to ensure that your site is secure, and an electronic certificate that authenticates your site so customers will know that the credit card data can be safely sent through the Internet.

• *Privacy*

More and more customers refuse to send personal data over the Internet unless they know how it will be used. Privacy policies need to be posted clearly on your store's pages.

• *Fraud*

Organizations need to be wary about the burgeoning increase of credit card fraud, particularly from purchases made from certain countries. Once an order is sent, it may be difficult if not impossible to get payment if the card was used fraudulently. Credit card companies often protect the consumer from fraud, but not the person or organization selling the goods.

E-COMMERCE STRATEGIES

Organizations can choose from among three strategies for creating an e-commerce presence on the Web. They can create the store using their own resources, hire someone else to design it, or pay a recurring fee to use a customizable template. These strategies are referred to, respectively, as "build," "buy," or "rent."

• *Build*

To build your own e-commerce store, you'll need a merchant account from a financial institution, shopping cart software, software that makes your site secure, tools for enhancing the appearance of your site, software to help you ship and track orders, and accounting software.

Almost all of these tools can be found online, and many can be obtained for free or at low cost. The main advantage of building is that you can customize your site and make changes without having to rely on third parties. You don't have to trust an application service provider with sensitive information, and you won't have anxiety about that provider going belly up, as many did during the dot-com feeding frenzy at the turn of the 21st century.

Disadvantages include not having access to the technical assistance that's often available from a third party that builds your site, and the additional workload that comes with building and maintaining your site.

- *Buy*

For-profit providers have sprung up who are willing to design a customized e-commerce Web site for you. The advantage is that you don't have to do much work. The main disadvantage is that such services can be costly, and you may need to depend on a third party for technical assistance.

- *Rent*

Other for-profit providers have developed a template for Web sites that can be customized to your needs. Typically, the e-commerce site resides on the server of the provider, but is seamlessly integrated with your organization's site. You pay a recurring fee.

The advantage is that if you decide to exit, you haven't lost much of an upfront investment compared to building or buying. Again, you have to trust that provider who rents you the site to stay in business, keep your information confidential, and provide any technical assistance and support services you need.

Which option you choose depends on many factors,

including how much money you're willing to invest, your comfort level with outside providers having access to sensitive information, your need for technical support, your ability to "do it yourself," and whether you have the time to devote to building or maintaining a site.

OTHER BUSINESS MODELS

In addition to this traditional online store model, several other nonprofit e-commerce models have developed, and more are likely to emerge. Among the best known are these:

Online shopping mall

A for-profit provider enters into an agreement with your organization to pay you a commission on purchases made by your organization's constituency from a range of online retailers and discounters.

Your organization advertises the availability of the program on your Web site and other promotional materials.

Online Charitable Auction

Either using your own software or the services of a turnkey application service provider, your organization offers donated goods and services for auction. Unlike face-to-face auctions, online auctions are able to be conducted 24 hours a day, offer an unlimited number of items, permit people to participate who are on the other side of the globe, and the work to set up and administer the auction can be performed by "virtual" volunteers.

Affiliate Programs

Pioneered by Amazon.com, an affiliate program generally consists of placing a piece of computer code on your Web site, provided by the provider, that links to that provider. When someone clicks on that link and purchases a product or service from the provider, your organization receives a commission.

Affiliate Online Stores

There are for-profit providers that will partner with your organization to offer generic products, such as mugs, T-shirts, and even stuffed bears emblazoned with your organization's logo.

You send your logo to the provider and advertise the availability of these products. Those interested in purchasing them click on a link on your site, which takes them to the online store of the provider.

Your organization receives a commission and doesn't have to make an investment in making the products or storing the inventory, or handling any of the transactions.

CONCLUSION

With competition for gifts and grants increasing, e-commerce offers opportunities for nonprofit organizations to generate revenues.

While there are some risks involved and startup costs in time and money, many organizations find that the benefits outweigh the costs.

Those that fail to respond to this trend and take advantage of what e-commerce has to offer will literally be missing a golden opportunity.

21

Fund Raising's 20 Biggest and Costliest Mistakes

Call them what you will - gaffes, blunders, oversights, or errors - mistakes creep into everyone's professional life. But in fund raising - unlike other fields - where thousands if not millions of dollars are often at stake, mistakes can be especially hazardous.

Who hasn't forfeited a significant gift, or received but a token one, due to some serious miscalculation?

While there may be hundreds of them, 20 potentially costly fund raising mistakes stand out. They can't really be ranked, since circumstances alter their impact. But here they are in an effort to ward you away from them.

■ **Thinking your organization will attract support simply because it's a good cause**

Just because you have a good cause -- one of thousands, really -- doesn't mean money will wend its way to you.

Organizations must attract support the old fashioned way

-- earn it.

Giving away money is something we all do reluctantly, and it's hardly an instinctive act. Nonetheless, people will support you if you present them with a challenging project that is consistent with their interests.

To succeed, you must explain exactly why you seek the funding, why your project is compelling, who will benefit, and why the money is needed now.

In other words, your needs -- presented as opportunities -- must be specific, people-oriented, and have a sense of urgency.

Keep in mind, always, that people give in order to get. They don't simply want to give away their money, they want to feel they're investing it and getting something in return.

■ Thinking that others can raise the money

Successful fund raising abides by the "rock in the pond" principle. That is, you can't expect others to contribute until those closest to the center of your organization do so. The farther from the center, the weaker the interest.

In short, solicitation starts with your inner "family" -- most notably the board. Only when these individuals have made proportionately generous contributions, do you reach out to your external constituency.

Why this principle? Because it only makes sense that if a board approves a program involving significant outlays, with the understanding that money has to be raised, then these same trustees must commit themselves to giving and getting.

If your governing body won't do so, who will?

■ Believing that because people are wealthy they will contribute to you

Simply because someone is wealthy, or thought to be

wealthy, is no reason to assume that he or she will want to give to your project. This is the thinking of neophytes.

People make gifts, substantial gifts that is, only after you've reached out, informed them of your work, *and* meaningfully involved them in your organization.

It is then that the prospective donor understands your goals, recognizes their importance, and welcomes the opportunity to have an impact.

Solicitation rightfully becomes the final step in the fund raising process, not the first one.

■ Thinking you can whisk wealthy prospects in at the last minute

Individuals, if they are to be committed to your organization, must have the opportunity to be involved in your work -- and not at the 11th hour.

Intensively courting prospects just prior to your fund raising drive is an insulting ploy, and most are smart enough to know what you're up to.

Much more advisable is to continuously involve prospects, for just as the best trustees are those who are meaningfully involved, the best contributors -- and best solicitors, too -- are involved in your drive from conception to victory.

Dollars, as Jerold Panas notes, follow commitment. And commitment follows involvement.

■ Failing to research and evaluate prospects

Rarely do meaningful gifts come from strangers. Most major donors are either associated with an organization or have logical reasons to give.

It is the role of prospect research to reveal these logical reasons by focusing on three elements, namely, linkage, ability, and interest.

Is there any link between the prospective donor and your organization? If so, then this link -- and it must be legitimate -- makes an appointment with the prospect possible.

Next is the person's ability to give. Does the prospect have enough discretionary income to justify your soliciting him or her for a major gift? Research will tell you the answer.

Finally, what is the prospect's interest in your organization? If he or she has little interest or limited knowledge about you, then you will likely receive a small gift if any at all.

■ Failing to ask

Very often, when campaigns fail, it's not because people didn't give, it's because they weren't asked. In fund raising, asking is the name of the game.

The problem is, only for the rarest person is asking for a gift easy. For most of us, the discomfort is so strong we'll invent 100 excuses to procrastinate.

Despite any training, despite any inspirational send-off, asking will always be the biggest challenge.

What can temper the fear to some degree is keeping in mind that prospects, who are usually more sensitive than we expect, respond favorably to solicitors who are dedicated and genuinely enthusiastic about the cause they represent.

■ Thinking that publicity will raise money

Publicity, despite our best wishes, doesn't raise money.

If you have solicitors and prospects, a strong case, and a campaign plan, you won't need any publicity.

Those who do insist on a big splash are, more often than not, people who don't want to face the rigors of a campaign. When the publicity push fails to create a stir, they use it as an excuse for not working.

As for campaign materials, most serious donors see them as non-essential. They much prefer a persuasive verbal presentation, underscored by simple documentation.

So long as you treat your press releases, brochures, drawings, or photographs as aids and not as solicitation devices, they will be useful but they will never take the place of direct asking.

■ Failing to recruit the right trustees

Of all the groups important to an organization, none is more vital than the board of directors.

There are exceptions, to be sure, but in 99 out of 100 cases an organization which consistently attracts the funding it needs has a board that accepts fund raising as a major responsibility, despite any other governing duties.

Put another way, an organization's ability to raise money is almost always in direct proportion to the quality and dedication of its leadership.

As Hank Rosso, founder of the Fund Raising School puts it, "People who have the fire of leadership burning within their souls, and who have that deep commitment to the organization's mission, will drive any program through to success."

■ Believing you can raise money by the multiplication table

People new to fund raising often get it in their heads that all you have to do is divide your goal by the number of likely donors, then ask everyone to give an equal amount.

But you can't raise money adequately by the multiplication table -- trying, for instance, to get 1,000 persons to give $1,000.

There are several inherent problems here. First, not every-one will give (which throws a wrench into the whole ap-proach). Second, we all tend to give in relation to others. If someone, five times wealthier than you, pledges $1,000, are you likely to feel a $1,000 pledge from you is fair? Third, seeking $1,000 from each donor in effect sets a ceiling on what an unusually generous person might wish to pledge.

■ Failing to have deadlines

By nature most of us are procrastinators, and whatever we have plenty of time to do, well, we seldom get it done.

For many if not most volunteers, the thought of asking someone for a contribution leads to procrastination.

To counter this, you must press for specific accomplish-ments within prescribed deadlines. In other words, to force action you need a campaign schedule with target dates understood by all.

Everyone will then know the rules of the game and, despite the pressure, will be grateful for the deadline.

■ Failing to have a strong rationale

Before setting out to raise money, each organization must think through the rationale for its appeal: why do the funds need to be raised, what will they achieve, and who will benefit?

The mere fact that you and your board need money won't stir people, no matter how well organized your effort.

Rather, with your case for support you must move your prospects emotionally and intellectually. They need to feel that, by contributing to your organization, life will in some way be better for them, for their children and grandchildren. They need to sense that their community -- or even the nation

- will be advanced as a result.

■ Failing to cultivate donors

Cultivation, a sustained effort to inform and involve your prospects, is needed for practically every gift -- the bigger the gift, usually the more preparatory steps needed.

The best cultivation, which uses a mixture of printed matter, special events, and personal attention, takes place slowly over a period of time, sometimes years.

If there's any secret to it, it is being yourself and cultivating people the way you would want to be cultivated. That is, with simple sincerity not glitzy programs.

Donors give more when they can visualize an organization not as an organization but as people. Achieving that end is, in essence, the goal of all successful cultivation programs.

■ Failing to set a realistic goal

In all but the newborn nonprofit, it's a mistake at the outset of a campaign to say, "We'll raise as much as we can."

This often reveals to prospective donors that your board or staff haven't analyzed the organization's needs.

Rather, a tenable dollar goal emanates out of your organization's growth pattern and the (evaluated) financial ability of your prospect list. It is not, as some assume, simply a percentage increase over last year's gross, nor is it necessarily the difference between the total dollars you need, less expected income.

While some argue for a high goal, and others insist on a low, achievable one, what really is desired is that magic number that inspires your volunteers, makes them work harder than they expected, and gives them the unmatched thrill of victory.

■ Failing to adequately train solicitors

No matter how virtuous your project or organization, most prospects need to be sold on contributing. You must, therefore, have a team of highly trained solicitors -- a "sales force" if you will.

Generally, you'll be dealing with three types of volunteers, each requiring slightly different treatment. First is the rookie who wants to help but needs detailed instructions. Second is the veteran of many campaigns who needs special prodding to attend trainings. And third is *every* volunteer who's being introduced to new procedures.

No matter how bright or experienced your volunteers, nor how busy they are, too many drives degenerate due to mediocre solicitor training.

■ Failing to thank your donors

Thanking donors, besides being polite, is an act of cultivation - and a smart one.

People appreciate when their generosity is recognized. They not only feel closer to your organization, they're inclined to continue giving.

Most important with thank-you's is to acknowledge gifts positively and quickly. You want the donor to know that your trustees are aware of the gift, that his or her generosity will stir others to give, and that your organization you will put the money to good use.

Board members can be especially effective in expressing appreciation, either by sending notes or by making telephone calls to selected donors.

■ Failing to focus on your top prospects first

It is foolish to squander your efforts on small donors until you've approached all of your best prospects.

This is of course known as *sequential* solicitation.

You begin by seeking the largest gift first - the one (at the top of your gift table) that is needed to make your campaign a success.

If this top gift comes in at the level you require, then it will set the standard and all other gifts will relate to it.

If it's too low, other gifts will drop accordingly and possibly imperil your whole campaign.

Sequential solicitation forces you to focus on your most promising prospects. While small donors are graciously treated, they do not receive disproportionate attention.

■ **Failing to ask for a specific gift**

The need to ask for a specific gift is one of the most misunderstood -- or it is feared? -- principles in raising money. "Will you join me in giving $500 to the Wakefield Symphony?" leaves no doubt as to the size of gift the solicitor is requesting.

Most prospective donors need and want guidance. By requesting a specific amount, you show that you've given thought to your drive and you put the prospect in a position of having to respond.

The suggested amount becomes a frame of reference, one that will get serious consideration if the solicitor is a friend, peer, or respected community figure.

■ **Failing to focus on the best sources and methods**

Nearly every board hopes it can raise the money it needs from foundations and businesses. These sources, perhaps because they're more impersonal, are seen as less scary than people.

And while, certainly, you want diversity in your funding, it's imperative that you and your board understand that most contributions -- fully 90 percent -- come from individuals. Here is where you'll invest your time and effort if you're serious.

As for methods, the most effective way of raising money -- and most productive in terms of the *size* of gifts -- is the face-to-face approach. The second most productive -- again in terms of the size of gifts -- is the appeal made to a small group of persons. The third most effective is the telephone call. And the least effective solicitation, in terms of gift size, is direct mail.

■ Failing to find the right person to ask

Find the right person to ask the right person is an old but enduring maxim in fund raising.

There will of course be exceptions, but a solicitor who makes a $100 commitment to your cause should call upon prospects who are capable of giving a similar amount. Likewise, a $500 prospect is best approached by a solicitor who himself has contributed a similar sum.

But as important as matching like amounts is pinpointing just the right solicitor. Some prospects expect to be asked by the president or the chairperson of the board. Others are less formal and would welcome the person they know best from the organization to ask for the gift. Still others may need the ego stroking of a team of solicitors. Reading this dynamic correctly is *the* key to success.

In a large campaign, solicitor/prospect matching can consume hours. But it is one of the very best uses of time.

■ Failing to see your top prospects in person

While there are dozens of ways to solicit prospects, nothing beats the personal request. The adage, "people give to people not to organizations," is another way of phrasing this principle.

Certainly if your organization has a favorable image it helps. But the personal request of a friend or peer for support has a far greater impact than any knowledge your prospect may have about you.

Harold Seymour, legendary fund raiser, puts it best: "For clinking money, you can shake the can. For folding money, you should go ask for it. For checks and securities and gifts in pledges, you have to take some pains - make the appointment, perhaps take someone along, count on making two or more calls, and in general give the process enough time and loving care to let it grow and prosper."

APPENDICES

Appendix I

Fund Raising Myths

Medicine has had its fill of them: Poor light weakens the eyes; tonsils must be removed; drafts cause colds.

So has popular culture: Santa Claus, Rip Van Winkle, and Nessie the Loch Ness Monster.

Myths surround us. Some are just plain kooky, others like chicken soup, well, maybe there's a grain of truth to them. When it comes to mistruths and fallacies, fund raising certainly has its share. Talk with board members, volunteers, or even some staff, and you'll be startled by some of the notions they hold.

Some, like those detailed below, have remarkable staying power.

- **Tax deductibility is a prime motivator**

While major donors will take full advantage of tax incentives, they are not the prime impetus behind big gifts. Donors give primarily because ... they are asked to, they play a leadership role in your organization, they believe in your goals, they seek recognition, peer pressure is exerted, there's a family tradition of giving, and other such reasons. Only after prospects have been motivated by one or more of these reasons do tax matters come into play.

Since gifts to thousands of organizations are tax-deductible, it's better to assume that this motive isn't a prime one for your prospects. What they care more about is the mission and function of your organization. Do everything you can to sell this feature. It is, after all, what truly distinguishes your organization.

- **Foundations and businesses are the prime targets**

As anyone who's been in development for long knows, the largest amount of money has always been contributed by private individuals.

Gifts by individuals comprise more than 90 percent of all funds contributed to nonprofits each year. The percent ebbs and flows only slightly.

While grants from foundations and corporations get greater visibility (what are PR staffs for anyway?), without the generosity of individual people our nation's churches, schools, hospitals, arts, and social welfare organizations could not exist. Given this reality, an organization should have no trouble knowing where to go for resources.

- **People will give because yours is a good cause**

Just because you have a good cause doesn't mean you'll attract support.

Giving away money, even for those who've lost count of theirs, is something done with great reluctance.

Still, people will support you if you present them with a challenging project that is consistent with their interests. To succeed, you must explain exactly why you seek the funding, why your project is compelling, who will benefit, and why the money is needed now.

Never assume, even among your inner circle, that your mission is self-evident. Explain - or, rather, sell it - again and again and again.

For no matter how enticing your project, no matter how skilled your solicitors, no matter how august your organization, your prospects must have an abiding belief in your organization's work if you are to succeed.

When you feel you've sold your mission with all the ardor you can muster, then you're ready to begin talking about your campaign project.

- **Outside help isn't needed**

Conducting a fund raising campaign, particularly a large capital drive, is a formidable task. Only inexperienced board members will think they have the time, know-how, and organizational skills to do all that's necessary.

Either that, or they'll think most of the work can be handled by staff.

Certainly, staff members might have the know-how and the skills, but given their regular responsibilities, they won't really have the time to give undivided attention to a major campaign.

The fact is, for a campaign goal of any size, a consultant is almost always needed.

The good professional will: uncover your strengths and weaknesses; help you screen and rate your inner group; develop a campaign master plan; help you build your strongest case; help you develop a prospect list; train you and your inner group to be effective solicitors; assist you in setting a goal.

Fees may be high initially, but the right consultant will prove to be a sound - and necessary - investment.

- ## You can hire somebody to raise big money

People new to fund raising often believe they can hire someone to enter the community, whip up a persuasive case, call upon potential donors, and deliver thousands if not millions of new dollars.

It doesn't work this way, of course.

Gifts, at least those of any consequence, come only with cultivation, and often the size of the gift reflects the time and care spent cultivating the prospective donor.

Moreover, in most successful campaigns, board members and the companies they manage or own contribute anywhere from 25 to 50 percent of the total campaign goal.

In short, people make substantial gifts only after you've reached out, informed them of your work, *and* meaningfully involved them in your organization. It is then that the prospective donor understands your goals, recognizes their importance, and welcomes the opportunity to have an impact. Solicitation becomes the final step in the fund raising process, not the first one.

- ## Publicity raises money

When it comes to seeking major gifts, the power of the written word is overrated.

As Jerold Panas, who has studied the subject points out, very few donors act on printed brochures. It is the verbal presentation that makes the difference. Indeed, many gifts are made without any campaign material at all.

Why, then, do thousands of organizations waste millions of dollars annually on fund raising materials that are of marginal value. Probably because volunteers and staff hope to avoid the discomfort of facing the prospect and asking for a gift. Carefully prepared materials can create a good impression, illustrate urgent needs, and legitimize the appeal for prospects. But always such materials must serve as *supporting pieces*, never taking the place of direct, eyeball to eyeball contact.

- **You don't need a feasibility study**

A feasibility study, conducted properly, does much more than help you set a dollar goal. It thoroughly examines your organization and your ability to raise money.

Is your board effective? How many donors do you have? Have these donors been increasing? How much volunteer leadership is available? What are the skills of your staff, especially those related to fund raising. What records do you have?

Moreover, how is your organization viewed in the community? Is it well known? Are your services considered important? Who might be the best leaders for your campaign? Are they available? Is this a good time to raise capital funds? Are the community's well-heeled residents inclined to contribute? If not, why not? Considering the importance of these and many other questions, many organizations won't proceed with a campaign until a feasibility study is conducted. Certainly it can be a safeguard against launching a campaign destined to fail.

- **Prospective donors are unlike you and me**

Perhaps the best way to think about your potential donors is to think about yourself, because you too are a prospect for someone's campaign.

Just like you, your prospects are interested in improving their community. They care about others. They're sensitive. And, like most of us, they're busy, which is why you want to approach them honestly and directly.

If you're dedicated and genuinely excited about your

cause, they'll sense it and respond favorably.

Treat your prospects like regular people. Don't tread gingerly nor be over-solicitous. And you needn't worry about asking for too much. Your prospects won't be embarrassed. They may not give what you want, but they know what things cost these days. And they'll respect your request.

Anytime you wonder how to deal with a prospect, put yourself in his or her place. Ask yourself how you'd want to be treated and you'll have your answer.

• Knowing your prospect is wealthy is enough

If a prospect you've identified is wealthy, does that mean he or she will, as a matter of course, give to your organization? Of course not. Ability to give doesn't necessarily equate with desire to give.

To earn support, you must induce in your prospect the *desire* to give. That takes cultivation. And cultivation, which can continue for years, begins with getting to *know* your prospect. The more you know, the better chance you have of attracting the support you want.

Make a concerted effort to learn as much as you can about your prospect's philanthropic, business, and social habits. Find out which organizations he or she belongs to; where the prospect contributes; his or her interests and hobbies; the interests of the immediate family; and the social affiliations of the prospect.

After gathering this data, ask yourself which of your projects might interest him or her, might bring the prospect into your organization.

If you see a match, then set about designing an effective cultivation program.

- **Others are more comfortable soliciting**

The truth is almost everyone finds it difficult, if not impossible, to ask for a contribution.

For board members, the anxiety can be so great that excuse upon excuse is offered for not getting involved. What this usually means, natural fear notwithstanding, is that they don't understand the importance of taking a leadership role in fund raising.

But board members must blaze the trail in fund raising. They own the organization; they are responsible for its well-being and success. If they, who set policy and govern the organization, won't take a lead role in fund raising, why would anyone else? Moreover, unless every trustee participates in fund raising, resentments will inevitably arise. Those who raise money will resent those who set policy.

Despite any and all rationalizations, everyone who believes in the organization can and should participate fully in fund raising.

- **Your goal is simply the amount you need**

It's usually a mistake to set a goal based simply upon what you need. Very often, especially for newer organizations, what you need is much more than you can hope to raise.

Instead, consider this rule of thumb.

Generally speaking, the 10 largest gifts to your campaign will add up to approximately one-third to one-half of the amount you can raise.

Therefore, if you're fairly confident you can raise $50K from your top group - that is, your board and inner circle - it's not unreasonable to assume that, with considerable effort, you should be able to raise $100K to $150K.

Of course, other factors will help you set a realistic goal as well. Have you done a feasibility study and, if so, what did it suggest? How much did your most recent campaign raise? What do your prospect ratings show? Are your campaign leaders capable of uncovering unexpected money?

These are all factors that must be weighed before you arrive at an estimate of how much you think you can raise.

• A capital campaign will hurt your annual drive

Not necessarily, and sometimes just the opposite. Granted, it can be difficult to conduct both campaigns in the same year.

Some organizations are so daunted by the challenge that, rather than ask annual donors for two pledges (one annual, one capital) at approximately the same time, they include, as a part of their capital campaign goal, the funds they'd normally raise for annual operating expenses.

Other organizations shun this approach and continue their annual giving as a separate program. They in fact believe annual giving increases as a result of the capital drive, partly because donors are asked to increase their annual gifts, but also because the excitement surrounding a capital campaign often prompts higher giving.

As for which approach is best for you, circumstances and experience will dictate that.

• The wells of philanthropy will soon dry up

Americans are noted for their generosity, but we don't give away nearly much as we could. How many of us contribute even a fraction - say, two percent - of our income to worthy causes? How many people really give sacrificially?

Granted, the climate is competitive, but all this means is you have to work hard to elevate your campaign, to make it a top priority among your potential supporters.

To do this, you must be able to persuasively communicate why your appeal needs to take place; what you will achieve if your drive is successful; and the people who will benefit. It's not so much that money is short, ideas are. Says George Brakeley, Jr., "There are uninvited billions to be raised out there. Your job is to invite them in."

- **The condition of the economy is critical**

The condition of the economy is no reason to delay your campaign. For even in periods of financial distress, philanthropy inches forward or at worst plateaus temporarily.

Giving is a part of our ethos. So long as you run a healthy organization that makes a difference in people's lives, Americans will dig deep to support you.

As the president of one America's oldest fund raising counseling firms pointed out years ago, there is little or no evidence that the ups and downs of the stock market appreciably affect giving.

In fact, during poor economic conditions major donors often respond with greater generosity.

Appendix II

What Board Members Must Know to Succeed

Hundreds of books have been written on the subject of fund raising, and hairs have been split on virtually every principle and technique.

Professionals in the field use these works to hone their skills, but board members neither have the time nor the inclination to make a concerted study of the subject. Instead, they need the essence, the collective wisdom, of what works and doesn't work, especially as it pertains to their role in fund raising.

To this end, the following 48 maxims, written specifically with board members in mind, are presented.

• The mission and goals must be clear

Before you begin any fund raising drive, you must know your organization's purpose. Granted, your goals are in your mission statement, but are they still valid? Are your objectives current and credible? Your prospective donors will ask you about them and you must be prepared to respond.

• Fund raising is the board's responsibility

The board of directors is charged with governing the organization and ensuring that it's mission is carried out. That responsibility necessarily includes finding the resources to carry out that mission. To view this as the role of others is illogical. Organizations which attract funding have boards that accept fund raising as a major responsibility.

• You can't hire it out

Those untutored in fund raising often believe they can hire someone to enter the community, call upon prospects, and deliver bags of new money. It doesn't work that way, of course. People make substantial gifts only after you've reached out, informed them of your work, *and* meaningfully involved them in your organization.

• Recruit the right trustees in the beginning

When a board is weak in fund raising, it usually means its members weren't recruited properly. If you expect a board member to raise money and make a significant gift, you have to say so up front. Include in your orientation a segment on development, during which you explain the role board members are expected to play.

• Don't venture out before you're ready

To determine your readiness for serious fund raising, you'll have to answer some tough questions: Does your organization really know itself? Do you have a history of philanthropic support? Is your organization viewed favorably in the community? Do board members agree the cause is worthwhile? Is your case compelling? Do you have the required leadership?

- **Select the best possible leadership**

Recruiting top leadership is probably the most important ingredient in fund raising. For each individual you're considering, ask yourself the following: Is this individual respected by colleagues? Does he or she have the stature to attract others. Will this person give and at what level? Will he or she solicit others? Will the person devote the necessary time?

- **Include your best prospective donors**

To succeed in fund raising, you will usually depend on a small number of major gift prospects; and the way to attract their support is to *involve* them from the inception of your program. Ask them to serve on major committees, see that they attend strategy sessions, and thoroughly inform them of your goals.

- **Staff leadership is critical**

Big givers respond to strong and capable staff leadership. In fact, the staff leadership of an organization is one of the core factors in motivating a gift, according to author Jerold Panas. If prospects are turned off or don't have a high regard and respect for those running the show, especially the chief executive officer, they won't give.

- **You must have a strong case**

Before setting out to raise money, you must think through the rationale for your appeal: why do you need the funds, what will they achieve, and who will benefit? Your case for support must move prospects emotionally and intellectually. They need to feel that if they contribute life in some way will be better for them and their community.

- ### Recruit an ample number of volunteers

The chairperson and board development committee can't carry the full load of fund raising. Volunteers are needed who accept the responsibility and share in the planning. This means more than soliciting, however, for volunteers should help rate prospects, plan the best approach to them, help set a goal, and be involved in nearly every aspect of campaign preparation.

- ### Fund raising training does help

You may be committed to your cause, but chances are you don't know how to ask for a gift. Be open, therefore, to learning some simple techniques: how to get the appointment, make the case, ask for the gift, and close. Don't assume you know how to ask even when you've been involved in previous campaigns.

- ### You have to spend money to raise money

Some major organizations can raise funds (capital funds) for as little as three percent of the goal. Other organizations, particularly small ones, may spend upwards of 50 percent. Many factors come into play: the amount you're trying to raise; the number of prospects; your plans for cultivation; professional counsel; and the length of your drive.

- ### Use professional counsel when necessary

Few organizations have the professional staff needed to conduct, or to give undivided attention to, a major fund raising campaign. Whereas a fund raising counselor can step in and develop a plan, conduct a feasibility study, help build the strongest case, suggest the goal, outline the leadership and volunteer needs, and establish a timetable and a realistic budget.

- **Concentrate your efforts on individuals**

Gifts by individuals (including bequests) comprise about 90 percent of all funds contributed to nonprofits each year. The percent ebbs and flows only slightly. While grants from foundations and corporations get greater visibility, without the generosity of individual donors our country's churches, schools, hospitals and social welfare organizations couldn't exist.

- **Set a realistic goal**

In setting a campaign goal, you must strike a balance between the needs of your organization and the perceived wherewithal of your constituents. As such, a realistic goal is based upon three factors: your need for funds; the perception of your organization and people's appreciation for your achievements; your campaign organization, that is, your plans, leadership, and staffing.

- **Don't count on windfall gifts**

While a carefully planned and orchestrated campaign will often produce a few windfall gifts, only the soft-headed anticipate these pleasant surprises. Should mega gifts come your way, rejoice. But if they don't, your well-conceived and well-executed campaign will raise money anyway.

- **Set deadlines**

By nature most of us are procrastinators. When we have plenty of time to do something we seldom get it done. Add to this our dislike of asking others for money and you have a prescription for delay. To counter this, you must press for specific accomplishments within prescribed time frames - a campaign schedule with agreed target dates.

- **Publicity won't raise money**

Thousands of organizations waste millions of dollars on fund raising materials - all because volunteers (and staff) hope to avoid the discomfort of facing the prospect and asking for a gift. Tasteful materials can create a good impression, illustrate needs, and legitimize the appeal, but always they must serve as *supporting pieces*, never taking the place of direct confrontation.

- **Know your prospect**

Most major donors are either associated with an organization or have logical reasons to give. It is the role of prospect research to uncover these reasons by focusing on: linkage, ability, and interest. Is there any link between the prospect and your organization? Does the prospect have enough discretionary income? And just what is the prospect's interest in your organization?

- **Rate the giving potential of your prospects**

Before embarking on a fund raising campaign, you must identify where most of the funds will come from. This is accomplished by a committee - of peers - "rating" prospects and assigning a gift range to each. Rating allows you to target your best prospects, helps you set your goal, and lets your prospect know what commitment you're seeking.

- **Solicit your natural prospects first**

It is folly to expect others to invest in your organization unless and until those closest to it do so. Known as the "rock in the pond" principle, this means board members, administrative staff, and other inner-family groups contribute first. You work from the center out, and the farther you go, the weaker the interest will be.

- **Solicit your best big-gift prospects first**

Don't expend effort on small donors until you've approached your best prospects. This is known as sequential solicitation. You begin by seeking the largest gift first. If this comes in at the level you require, then it will set the standard and all other gifts will relate to it. If it's too low, other gifts will drop accordingly.

- **Those who already give are the best prospects**

To succeed in raising big money, you must have an active fund raising program in place. Which is to say, without a constituency who is already cultivated and giving, your chances for raising serious money are slim. Donors rarely make major gifts without some prior experience of giving to your organization.

- **Make asking your last step**

The *final*, and not the first, step in fund raising is asking. This may surprise those who think solicitation alone IS fund raising. But only after a series of earlier steps have been followed does asking come easily. It is then the prospect is meaningfully involved, understands your goals, appreciates their importance, and welcomes the chance to invest.

- **Friends, not enemies**

Too many people think of fund raising as a "hard sell." But it's more appropriate to see yourself as a friend to the prospect, trying to help him or her do something of consequence. Your job isn't to convince people of what they *should* do, it is to relate the aims of your organization to what they already want.

- **When envisioning a prospect, think of yourself**

Except that they may be wealthier, prospects are just the same as you. They're interested in helping, they don't like gimmicks or dishonesty. Prospects respond favorably to direct approaches, to solicitors who are genuinely enthusiastic about their causes, and they won't be embarrassed if you ask them for too much.

- **You must cultivate**

A sustained effort to inform and involve your prospects is needed for practically every gift - the bigger the gift, the more preparatory steps needed. The best cultivation, which uses a mix of printed matter, special events, and personal attention, takes place slowly over a period of time, sometimes years.

- **You can't whisk in wealthy prospects**

Intensively courting prospects just prior to your campaign is an insulting and ineffective ploy. More advisable is to continuously involve prospects, for just as the best trustees are those who are meaningfully involved, the best contributors - and best solicitors - are involved in your drive from conception to victory.

- **Worthiness of your cause isn't enough**

Giving away money is something everyone does with reluctance. Still, people will give if you present them with a challenging project in which they have some interest. To succeed, you must explain why you seek the funding, why your project is compelling, who will benefit, and why the money is needed now.

- **Don't overwork your solicitors**

One solicitor personally calling upon five prospects is a standard measure in fund raising. Solicitors asked to do more will usually procrastinate; worse, they may telephone or write to their prospects. Beware of well-meaning people who offer to take more assignments. While they may make the calls, they will tend to do so hastily and without much enthusiasm.

- **Carefully match solicitors and prospects**

Generally speaking, a solicitor who makes a $100 gift should call upon prospects capable of giving similar amounts. Likewise, a $500 prospect is best approached by a $500 solicitor. Pinpointing just the right solicitor is vital too. Some prospects expect to be asked by the president, others would welcome the person they know best from your organization, still others need the ego-stroking of a team of solicitors.

- **Make your contribution first**

As Socrates said, "Let him that would move the world first move himself." In fund raising, this means solicitors must give before asking others to do so. When a solicitor embarks without having contributed, not only does she solicit with less conviction but she's vulnerable to the charge, "Why should I give if you, who are close to the organization, haven't?"

- **Giving must be proportionate**

You can't raise money adequately by the multiplication table - trying, for instance, to coax a thousand people to give $1,000. First, not everyone will give. Second, if someone with far greater wealth gives $1,000, would an equal pledge from you be fair? Third, seeking identical amounts sets a ceiling on what a generous person might wish to pledge.

- **See your top prospects in person**

The best way to raise money is to ask for it and the best

method to use is person-to-person. But how often this vital principle is neglected by staff and volunteers. Inclement weather, aches and pains, too harried at the office, yesterday's rejection - all of these can prevent a reluctant fund raiser from making personal calls.

- **Use teams when soliciting**

It's almost always a good idea to solicit major gifts in teams: volunteer and CEO, volunteer and staff member, CEO and staff member. Team members not only reinforce each other, they're usually better equipped to answer questions and raise important points. Of course, when using the team approach, make sure all participants are following the same solicitation plan.

- **Translate the funds you seek into human terms**

Whatever cause you're raising money for, make your project personal for your prospect. A library isn't a collection of books; it's a fertile place where young minds grow. Cancer research isn't equipment and test tubes; it's the promise of a cure. Use a little imagination and translate your request into something people can identify and connect with.

- **Prospects are interested in their needs, not yours**

Notwithstanding the worthiness of your cause, prospects will be more likely to give when they see a benefit for themselves. Imagine your donors as customers. Customers aren't interested in helping a business prosper. They're interested in low prices, quality, convenience, and service. In sum, they're interested in what *they* need.

- **Present a specific figure to your prospects**

Most prospective donors want guidance. They want to

know how much you *hope* they'll give. By requesting a specific amount, rather than "whatever you can do," you show you've given thought to your campaign and you put the prospect in a position of having to respond. You provide a frame of reference, in other words.

• **Make it easy to contribute**

Most donors will give more if they know they can spread their gift over a period of years. By being flexible and offering donors a combination of devices, you'll encourage greater generosity. Make available installment pledges. Accept gifts of appreciated securities, trusts, real estate, and insurance. And consider a program of named commemorative opportunities.

• **Make sure you actually ask for the gift**

A campaign will be hurt more by those who would have said yes but were not asked, than by those who say no. Too often the cardinal rule of sales - ask for the order - is overlooked. The solicitor makes a superb presentation but when the time comes to ask, the mouth fills with cotton.

• **Have the courage to be silent**

The person who won't stop talking is the most unconvincing solicitor in the world. Silence not only gives the prospect a turn, it also puts everything squarely on his or her shoulders. He has to respond, if only to raise objections that you must address. Fight the natural urge to fill in uncomfortable silences.

• **Be reluctant to accept a small gift**

Since asking provokes anxiety, some solicitors are so relieved once they've asked that they'll take any gift, even if the $50,000 prospect offers $5,000. But the role of the solicitor is also one of negotiator. If a low amount is offered, stress again the importance of the project and describe how you, the solicitor, have given at a significant level for this very reason.

• One visit isn't enough

If you're seeking a significant gift, almost always you'll have to make several calls upon your prospect. In fact, it's practically a given that you won't receive a large gift during your first visit. Selling the drama, the power, and the excitement of your organization is the charge at your first meeting.

• Once you have the pledge, be off

Conclude the visit with your prospect as soon as you receive the pledge or gift. Otherwise, like a rookie salesperson you might "unsell" the customer with a verbal miscue. Since the purpose of your call is fulfilled when the commitment is made, thank the donor and leave immediately.

• Thank your donors

Beside being polite, thanking donors is an act of cultivation. Not only will your donors feel closer to you, they will continue giving. Most important is to acknowledge gifts positively and quickly. Let the donor know you're aware of the gift, that his or her generosity will prompt others to give, and that your organization will use the money wisely.

• Recognize your donors

While they may not ask for or seek it, appropriate recognition is welcomed and appreciated by major donors. However, it's up to the staff person to initiate the idea, encourage it, and review it with the donor. The dividends will be immense, especially as sincerely expressed gratitude is the first step in securing another and larger gift.

- **Don't fret timing**

Even in poor economic times, philanthropy inches forward or at worst plateaus. As long as you run a tight organization that makes a difference, people will support you. As the president of one of America's oldest fund raising counseling firms pointed out, there is little or no evidence that the ups and down of the stock market appreciably affect giving.

- **When all is said and done, keep it simple**

Keep in mind that, despite all principles and techniques, fund raising at heart is still quite simple. As author Irving Warner succinctly put it, "You raise money when you ask for it, preferably face-to-face, from the smallest possible number of people, in the shortest period of time, at the least expense."

The Triple Crown for Your Board

The Ultimate Board Member's Book
A 1-Hour Guide to Understanding Your Role and Responsibilities • *Kay Sprinkel Grace*

Here is a book for *all* nonprofit boards:
• Those wanting to operate with maximum effectiveness,
• Those needing to clarify exactly what their job is, and,
• Those wanting to ensure that all members — novice and veteran alike
— are 'on the same page' with respect to roles and responsibilities.

The Ultimate Board Member's Book will take your board members just one hour to read, yet they'll come away from it with a solid command of what they need to do to help your organization succeed.

It's all here in jargon-free language: how boards work, what the job entails, the time commitment, the role of staff, serving on committees and task forces, fundraising responsibilities, conflicts of interest, group decision-making, effective recruiting, board self-evaluation, and more.

Fund Raising Realities Every Board Member Must Face
1-Hour Crash Course on Raising Major Gifts for Nonprofit Orgs. • *David Lansdowne*

More than 25,000 board members and development officers across America have used the book, *Fund Raising Realities Every Board Member Must Face*, to help them raise substantial money for their organizations – especially as competition for the philanthropic dollar intensifies.

Hundreds of hospitals, colleges, museums, private schools, cultural organizations, and social service agencies have purchased a copy for every member of their board. In fact, David Lansdowne's book has become THE fastest selling fund raising book in America.

It's easy to see why. Have your board spend just *one* hour with this classic and they'll come to understand virtually everything they need to know about raising big gifts. Nothing more, nothing less.

Asking
A 59-Minute Guide to Everything Board Members, Volunteers, and Staff
Must Know to Secure the Gift • *Jerold Panas*

It ranks right up there with public speaking. Nearly all of us fear it. And yet it's critical to our success. *Asking for money*. It makes even the stout-hearted quiver. But now comes a book, *Asking: A 59-Minute Guide to Everything Board Members, Volunteers, and Staff Must Know to Secure the Gift*. And short of a medical elixir, it's the next best thing for emboldening you, your board members and volunteers to ask with skill, finesse … and powerful results.

What *Asking* convincingly shows — and one reason staff will applaud the book and board members will devour it — is that it doesn't take stellar communication skills to be an effective asker.

Nearly everyone, regardless of their persuasive ability, can become an effective fundraiser if they follow Jerold Panas' step-by-step guidelines.

Order from Emerson & Church, Publishers
Quantity Discounts Available • 508-359-0019

About the Author

David Lansdowne has spent his professional life in the nonprofit sector, serving in development and administrative positions for educational, cultural, and health organizations throughout America.